Nick Vandome

Photoshop Elements 10

eps

d Mac

In easy steps is an imprint of In Easy Steps Limited
4 Chapel Court · 42 Holly Walk · Leamington Spa
Warwickshire · United Kingdom · CV32 4YS

Notice of Liability
Every effort has been made to ensure that this book contains accurate
and current information. However, In Easy Steps Limited and the
author shall not be liable for any loss or damage suffered by readers
as a result of any information contained herein.

Trademarks
Photoshop® is a registered trademark of Adobe Systems Incorporated.
All other trademarks are acknowledged as belonging to their
respective companies.

In Easy Steps Limited supports The Forest Stewardship Council (FSC),
the leading international forest certification organisation. All our titles
that are printed on Greenpeace approved FSC certified paper carry the
FSC logo.

MIX
Paper from
responsible sources
FSC® C020837

Printed and bound in the United Kingdom

ISBN 978-1-84078-531-9

Contents

7 Layers 113

8 Text and Drawing Tools 125

9 Artistic Effects 145

1 Introducing Elements

Photoshop Elements is a digital image editing program that comprehensively spans the gap between very basic programs and professional-level ones. This chapter introduces the various sections and modes of Elements and shows how to access them. It also shows how to quickly get up and running with this powerful, flexible and creative image editing program.

About Elements

Photoshop Elements is the offspring of the professional-level image editing program, Photoshop. Photoshop is somewhat unusual in the world of computer software, in that it is widely accepted as being the best program of its type on the market. If professional designers or photographers are using an image editing program, it will almost certainly be Photoshop. However, two of the potential drawbacks to Photoshop are the cost (approximately $700) and its complexity. This is where Elements comes into its own. Adobe (the makers of Photoshop and Elements) have recognized that the majority of digital imaging users (i.e. the consumer market) want something with the basic power of Photoshop, but with enough user-friendly features to make it easy to use. With the explosion in the digital camera market, a product was needed to meet the needs of a new generation of image editors – and that product is Elements.

Elements contains the same powerful editing/color management tools as the full version of Photoshop and it also includes a number of versatile features for sharing images and for creating artistic projects, such as slide shows, cards, calendars and online photo albums. It also has valuable help features, such as the Guided Edit mode, which explains what different items can be used for and gives a step-by-step guide to various digital editing techniques:

Don't forget

Photoshop Elements can be bought online from Adobe and computer and software sites, or at computer software stores. There are Windows and Mac versions of the program.

Special effects

One of the great things about using Elements with digital images is that it provides numerous fun and creative options for turning mediocre images into eye-catching works of art. This is achieved through a wide variety of guided activities within Guided Edit:

Advanced features

In addition to user-friendly features, Elements also has more advanced functions, such as the histogram:

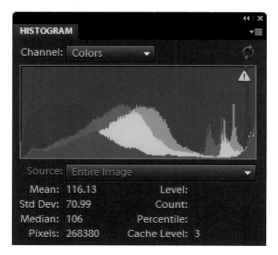

Don't forget

The histogram displays the tonal range of the colors in an image.

9

Welcome Screen

When you first open Elements, you will be presented with the Welcome Screen. This offers initial advice about working with Elements and also provides options for creating new files, or opening existing ones. The Welcome Screen appears by default but this can be altered once you become more familiar with Elements.

Welcome Screen functions

 Options for organizing photos, editing them and using them in a variety of creative ways

Hot tip

The Welcome Screen can be accessed at any time by selecting Window> Welcome from the Editor Menu bar.

 Click on the Top Features and What's New buttons to find out about certain functions in Elements

 Click on the Organize button to go to that area

 Click on the Edit button to go to that area

Editor Mode

From the Welcome Screen the Elements Editor interface can be accessed. This is a combination of the work area (where images are opened and edited), menus, toolbars, a toolbox and panels. At first it can seem a little daunting, but Elements has been designed to offer as much help as possible as you proceed through the digital editing process.

The components of the Elements Editor are:

Menu bar   Options bar   Shortcuts bar Panels bin

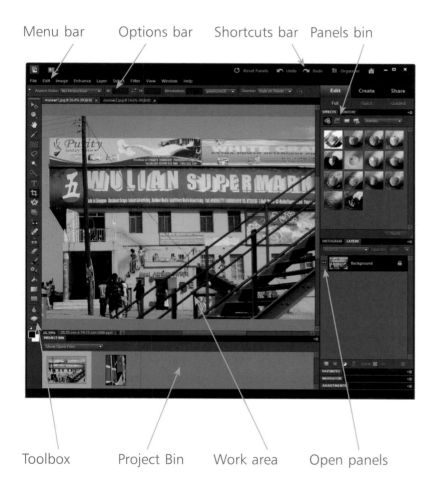

Toolbox   Project Bin   Work area   Open panels

Project Bin

The Project Bin is a feature that can be accessed from the Editor in either Full Edit or Quick Edit mode. The Project Bin enables you to quickly access all of the images that you have open within the Editor. To use the Project Bin:

1 Open two or more images. The most recently opened one will be the one that is active in the Editor

Hot tip

Images can also be made active for editing by dragging them directly from the Project Bin and dropping them within the Editor window.

2 All open images are shown here in the Project Bin

Hot tip

When an image has started to be edited, this icon appears on its top right-hand corner in the Project Bin.

3 Double-click on an image in the Project Bin to make that the active one for editing

12

Quick Edit Mode

Quick Edit mode contains a number of functions that can be selected from a panel and applied to an image, without the need to manually apply all of the commands. To do this:

 In the Editor, click on the Edit Quick button

Don't forget

For an in-depth look at Quick Edit mode, have a look at Chapter Four.

The currently active image is displayed within the Quick Edit window

Don't forget

The Project Bin is also available in Quick Edit and Guided Edit modes.

Select one of the commands to have it applied to the active image. This can either be applied by clicking on the Auto button or by dragging the appropriate slider to apply the command

Guided Edit Mode

Guided Edit mode is similar to Quick Fix mode, except that it focuses on common tasks for editing digital images and shows you how to perform them. To use Guided Edit mode:

1 In Edit mode, click on the Edit Guided button

Guided

2 The currently active image is displayed within the Guided Edit window

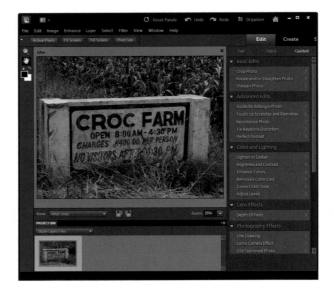

14

3 Select one of the actions that you want to perform. This will take you to a step-by-step process for undertaking the required action

▼ Advanced Edits

Guide for Editing a Photo   >
Touch Up Scratches and Blemishes   >
Recompose Photo   >
Fix Keystone Distortion   >
Perfect Portrait   >

Organizer Mode

The Organizer mode contains a number of functions for sorting, viewing and finding multiple images. To use the Organizer:

1 In Editor mode, click on the Organizer button

2 The Media Browser displays thumbnails of your photos, and also has functions for sorting and finding images

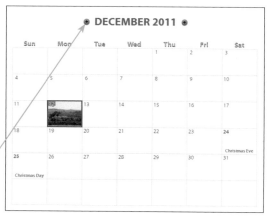

3 In the Media Browser, click on the Date View button

↶ Undo	↷ Redo	🖵 Display ▾
✓ Thumbnail View		Ctrl+Alt+1
Import Batch		Ctrl+Alt+2
Folder Location		Ctrl+Alt+3
Date View		Ctrl+Alt+D
🖳 View, Edit, Organize in Full Screen		F11
🖽 Compare Photos Side by Side		F12

4 This displays a calendar interface that can be used to view images that were captured on a specific date. Click here to move through the calendar

● DECEMBER 2011 ●

Sun	Mon	Tue	Wed	Thu	Fri	Sat
				1	2	3
4	5	6	7	8	9	10
11	12	13	14	15	16	17
18	19	20	21	22	23	24
						Christmas Eve
25	26	27	28	29	30	31
Christmas Day						

Create Mode

Create mode is where you can release your artistic flair and start designing items such as photo books and photo collages. It can also be used to create slide shows, create PhotoStamps and to put your images onto disc. To use Create mode:

1 In either the Editor or the Organizer, click on the Create button

2 Select one of the Create projects. Each project has a wizard that takes you through the create process

Don't forget

Create mode and Share mode can both be accessed from either the Editor or the Organizer in Elements. However, there are a few more options in both if they are accessed from the Organizer.

3 Create mode can be used to create a variety of artistic projects, containing your own images

Share Mode

Share mode can be used to distribute your images to family and friends in a variety of creative ways. To use Share mode:

1 In either the Editor or the Organizer, click on the Share button

2 Select one of the Share options

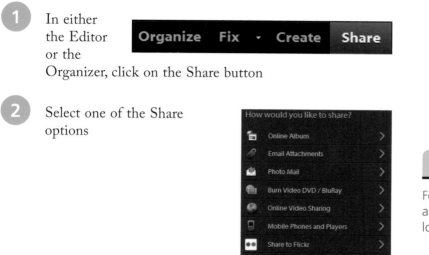

Don't forget

For a more in-depth look at Share mode have a look at Chapter Ten.

3 The projects have templates and wizards that take you through the process of creating the project for sharing

Menu Bar

In the Editor, the Menu bar contains menus that provide all of the functionality for the workings of Elements. Some of these functions can also be achieved through the use of the other components of Elements, such as the Toolbox, the Shortcuts bar, the Options bar and the panels. However, the Menu bar is where all of the commands needed for the digital editing process can be accessed in one place.

Menu bar menus

- File. This has standard commands for opening, saving and printing images, and also commands for creating Photomerge effects such as panoramas and combining exposures

- Edit. This contains commands for undoing previous operations, and standard copy and paste techniques

- Image. This contains commands for altering the size, shape and position of an image. It also contains more advanced functions, such as changing the color mode of an image

- Enhance. This contains commands for editing the color elements of an image. It also contains quick-fix options

- Layer. This contains commands for working with different layers within an image

- Select. This contains commands for working with areas that have been selected within an image, with one of the selection tools in the Toolbox

- Filter. This contains numerous filters that can be used to apply special effects to an image

- View. This contains commands for changing the size at which an image is displayed, and also options for showing or hiding rulers and grid lines

- Window. This contains commands for changing the way multiple images are displayed, and also options for displaying all of the components of Elements

- Help. This contains the various Help options

Don't forget

The Mac version of Elements also has a Photoshop Elements menu on the Menu bar. This contains the Preferences options.

Beware

Elements does not support the CMYK color model for editing digital images. This could be an issue if you use a commercial printer.

Toolbox

The Toolbox contains tools for adding items to an image (such as shapes and text), selecting areas of an image and also for applying editing techniques. Some of the tools have more than one option, in which case, they have a small black triangle at the bottom right of the default tool icon. To access additional tools in the Toolbox:

Click and hold here to access additional tools for a particular item

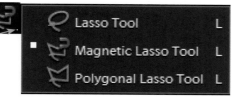

Working with the Toolbox

By default, the Toolbox is docked at the left of the main Editor window. However, it can be removed and dragged anywhere within the main window. To do this:

1 Click on the two arrows to view the Toolbox in one column. Click on the cross to close it

2 Click and drag here to move the Toolbox around the Editor window. Drag it back to its original location to redock it at the left of the window

Don't forget

The tools that have additional options are: the Marquee tools, the Lasso tools, the Magic Selection Brush tool, the Healing Brush tools, the Type tools, the Crop tools, the Eraser tools, the Brush tools, the Stamp tools, the Object tools (e.g. the Rectangle tool), the Blur tool and the Sponge tool.

Don't forget

For full details of the Toolbox functions, see the inside front cover of the book.

Hot tip

If the Toolbox is not visible, select Window> Tools from the Menu bar.

Options Bar

The Options bar provides attributes that can be set for a selected tool from the Toolbox. For instance, if the Eraser tool is selected, the Options bar offers choices for the type of eraser that can be used, its size, its mode and its opacity level. For each tool, a different set of options is available.

Using the Options bar

1 Click on a tool in the Toolbox (in this example it is the Magic Wand tool)

2 Select the options for the tool in the Options bar

3 Apply the tool to an image. The tool will maintain the settings in the Options bar until they are changed

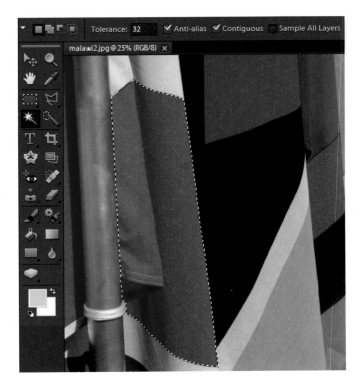

Panels

Elements uses panels to group together similar editing functions and provide quick access to certain techniques. The available panels are:

- Adjustments. This can be used to add or make editing changes to adjustment layers in the Layers panel

- Color Swatches. This is a panel for selecting colors that can then be applied to parts of an image or elements that have been added to it

- Content. This contains graphical elements that can be added to images. This includes backgrounds, frame shapes and artistic text

- Effects. This contains special effects and styles that can be applied to an entire image or a selected part of an image. There are also filters which have their own dialog boxes in which settings can be applied and adjusted. Layer Styles can also be applied to elements within an image

- Favorites. This is where favorite graphical elements from the Content panel can be stored and retrieved quickly

- Histogram. This displays a graph of the tonal range of the colors in an image. It is useful for assessing the overall exposure of an image and it changes as an image is edited

- Info. This displays information about an image, or a selected element within it. This includes details about the color in an image or the position of a certain item

- Layers. This enables several layers to be included within an image. This can be useful if you want to add elements to an existing image, such as shapes or text. Layers can also be used to merge two separate images together

- Navigator. This can be used to move around an image and magnify certain areas of it

- Undo History. This can be used to undo all, or some, of the editing steps that have been performed. Every action is displayed in the Undo History panel and these actions can be reversed by dragging the slider at the side of the panel upwards

Hot tip

The panels are located in the Panel Bin, which is at the right of the Editor window. This can be collapsed or expanded by selecting Window>Panel Bin from the Menu bar.

...cont'd

Working with panels

By default, all panels are minimized and grouped in the Panel Bin. However, it is possible to open one or more panels so that they are displayed independently from the Panel Bin. To work with panels:

1 Panels are grouped together in the Panel Bin at the right of the work area

2 Click and drag here to move a panel away from the bin (or move a detached panel back into the bin)

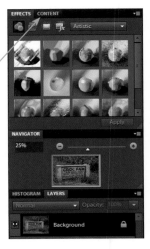

Beware

Don't have too many panels open at one time. If you do, the screen will become cluttered and it will be difficult to edit images effectively.

3 Click here on the top bar to expand or contract a panel

4 Every panel has its own menu; its options depend on the functions within the panel

Content Help
Help Contents

Small Thumbnail View
✓ Medium Thumbnail View
Large Thumbnail View

Apply

Close
Close Tab Group

Preferences

A number of preferences can be set within Elements to determine the way the program operates. It is perfectly acceptable to leave all of the default settings as they are, but as you become more familiar with the program you may want to change some of the preference settings. Preferences can be accessed by selecting Edit>Preferences from the Menu bar, and the available ones are:

- General. This contains a variety of options for selecting items, such as shortcut keys

- Saving Files. This determines the way Elements saves files

- Performance. This determines how Elements allocates memory when processing editing tasks. It also determines how Elements allocates disk space when processing editing tasks (scratch disks). If you require more memory for editing images (image editing can be a very memory-intensive process) you can do this by allocating up to four scratch disks on your hard drive. These act as extra areas from which memory can be used during the editing process

- Display & Cursors. This determines how cursors operate when certain tools are selected

- Transparency. This determines the color, or transparency, of the background on which an open image resides

- Units & Rulers. This determines the unit of measurement used by items, such as rulers

- Guides & Grids. This determines the color and format of any guides and grids that are used

- Plug-Ins. This displays any plug-ins that have been downloaded to enhance image editing with Elements

- Type. This determines the way text appears when it is added to images

- Organize & Share. These preferences open in the Organizer mode and offer a collection of preferences that are applicable to these functions. These are General, Files, Editing, Camera or Card Reader, Scanner, Date View, Keyword Tags and Albums, Sharing, Adobe Partner Services and Media-Analysis

Don't forget

Each preference has its own dialog box in which the specific preference settings can be made.

Don't forget

Guides and grids can be accessed from the View menu in Editor mode.

Hot tip

The Organize & Share preferences can be accessed by selecting Edit>Preferences from the Menu bar in either the Editor or the Organizer.

Elements for the Mac

For some previous versions of Elements, there has not been complete synchronization between the Mac and Windows versions. With some releases the Mac version came out slightly later than the Windows ones and none of the Mac versions have had the Organizer integrated into them. However, with Elements 10 the Mac version has the same Organizer as the Windows version and the two are now virtually identical.

The Mac version has the same editing functions:

- Full Edit

- Quick Edit

- Guided Edit

The interface is also almost identical to the Windows version:

The two differences are the standard Mac buttons for (from left to right) close, minimize and expand an open window.

The other difference is the four icons at the top left of the Editor window. These are to (from left to right) open a new blank file, save, help and arrange open files.

Organizer

With Elements 10 the Organizer has been included with the Mac version. This has the same interface and functionality as the Windows version:

Create and Share

The Mac version also has the same options for the Create and Share sections as the Windows version:

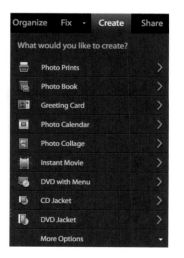

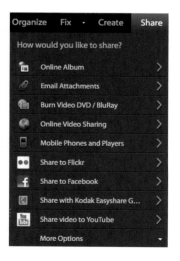

Getting Help

One of the differences between Elements and the full version of Photoshop is the amount of assistance and guidance offered by each program. Since Photoshop is aimed more at the professional end of the market, the level of help is confined largely to the standard help directory that serves as an online manual. Elements also contains this, but in addition it has the Getting Started option which is designed to take users through the digital image editing process as smoothly as possible. The Getting Started option offers general guidance about digital imaging techniques and there are also help items that can be accessed by selecting Help from the Menu bar. These include online help, information on available plug-ins for Elements, tutorials and support details.

Using the help files

Don't forget

For the Mac version of Elements the Help function can also be accessed from the Help button at the top of the Editor window.

1. Select Photoshop Elements Help from the Help menu and click Contents or Index. Then click once on an item to display it in the main window

2 Organizing Images

This chapter shows how to download digital images via Elements and then how to view, organize, compare and analyze them. It also shows how you can tag images, so that they are easy to find and how to search for items according to a variety of criteria such as by keywords or even individual objects within the images.

Obtaining Images

One of the first tasks in Elements is to download images so that you can start editing and sharing them. This can be done from a variety of devices, but the process is similar for all of them. To download images into Elements:

Don't forget

For a lot of digital cameras, the Photo Downloader window will appear automatically once the camera is connected to the computer. However, if this does not happen it will have to be accessed manually as shown here.

1 Access the Organizer by clicking on this button in the Editor

88 Organizer

2 Select File>Get Photos and Videos from the Menu bar and select the type of device from which you want to load images into Elements

📷 From Camera or Card Reader...	Ctrl+G
📠 From Scanner...	Ctrl+U
📁 From Files and Folders...	Ctrl+Shift+G
🔍 By Searching...	

Hot tip

Images can also be downloaded from existing files and folders on a computer. This means that they will be added to the Organizer's database and you will be able to apply all of its features to the images.

28

3 If you select From Camera and Card Reader, click under Get Photos From to select a specific device

Get Photos from:

-- Select a Device -- ▼

E:\<NIKON D70>
I:\<Camera or Card Reader>
< Refresh List >
-- Select a Device --

4 The images to be downloaded are displayed here, next to the device from which they will be downloaded

5 Click here to select a destination for the selected images and click the Get Photos button to download them

6 As the images are being downloaded, the following window is displayed

7 After the files have been copied they are then imported into Elements

8 Click on the Yes button so that the images are imported. They can then be viewed in the Organizer and opened in the Editor

Media Browser

The Media Browser is the function within the Organizer that is used to view, find and sort images. When using the Media Browser, images have to be actively added to it so it can then catalog them. Once images have been downloaded, the Media Browser acts as a window for viewing and sorting your images, no matter where they are located. Aspects of the Media Browser include the following:

1 Drag this slider to view images at different sizes in the Media Browser

2 Main window for viewing images

3 Options for adding tags to images and creating albums of similar images

4 Click here to select options for how images are displayed

↶ Undo	↷ Redo	▢ Display
✓ Thumbnail View		Ctrl+Alt+1
Import Batch		Ctrl+Alt+2
Folder Location		Ctrl+Alt+3
Date View		Ctrl+Alt+D
View, Edit, Organize in Full Screen		F11
Compare Photos Side by Side		F12

Magnification slider for changing the size at which images are viewed in the main window:

Accessing images

To access images within the Media Browser:

 1 Click on images to select them individually, or as a group

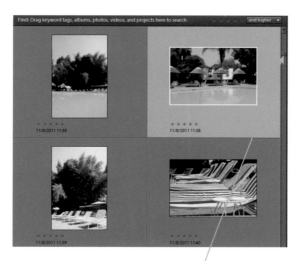

2 Drag here to scroll through images within the main window

3 Double-click on an image to view it in the whole Media Browser window

Full Screen Preview

From within the Media Browser it is possible to view all of your images, or a selection of them, at full screen size. In addition, music can be added to create an impressive slide show effect. To use the Full Screen Preview:

 In the Media Browser, click here and select View, Edit, Organize in Full Screen, or press F11

 The image is displayed, with the Quick Edit and Quick Organize panels displayed at the side of the window

Use these buttons to (from left to right) show or hide the filmstrip of images, show or hide the Quick Edit panel and show or hide the Quick Organize panel

Use these buttons to (from left to right) move to the previous image, play all images as a slide show and move to the next image

Use these buttons to (from left to right) view options for playing a slide show, select transitions for a slide show and view the general properties of an image

Full Screen Compare

In addition to viewing individual images at full screen size, it is also possible to compare two images next to each other. This can be a very useful way of checking the detail of similar images, particularly for items such as focus and lighting. To compare images using Full Screen Compare:

1 In Full Screen Preview, click here on the toolbar and select an option for comparing images

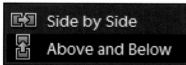

2 Click on two images in the image pane

3 Click on this button on the toolbar. This enables zooming on both images simultaneously

4 The images are displayed and the zoom command is applied to both of them

33

Auto-Analyzer

Once photos have been downloaded into the Organizer it is possible to run a function that analyzes several elements relating to the quality of the images. Once this has been done the elements are added as tags to the images. This creates a quick visual guide to the quality of photos, which can be viewed in the Organizer. To use the Auto-Analyzer:

34

1 In the Organizer, select the photos which you want to be analyzed. (If you do not select any images, the Auto-Analyzer will be performed over the whole collection)

2 Select Edit>Run Auto-Analyzer from the Menu bar. This will then be performed over the selected images (or the whole collection). Click on the OK button when the action has been completed

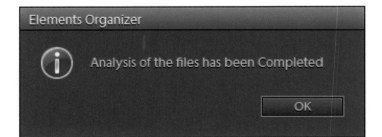

3 The Auto-Analyzer tags are added to the images

4 Double-click on an image

5 The tags that have been added are shown underneath the image. These are all elements that have been identified by the Auto-Analyzer

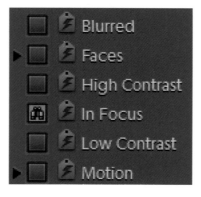

High Quality, Closeup, One Face, In Focus

6 The tags are automatically added to the Keywords Tag panel in the Organizer. Check on the box next to a tag to view all of the images with a specific tag

☐	🏷	Blurred
▶ ☐	🏷	Faces
☐	🏷	High Contrast
🔍 ☐	🏷	In Focus
☐	🏷	Low Contrast
▶ ☐	🏷	Motion

Beware

The Auto-Analyzer isn't infallible and sometimes it will identify elements that are not there, such as faces.

35

Stacks

Since digital cameras make it quick, easy and cheap to capture dozens, or hundreds, of images on a single memory card it is no surprise that most people are now capturing more images than ever before. One result of this is that it is increasingly tempting to take several shots of the same subject, just to try and capture the perfect image. The one drawback with this is that when it comes to organizing your images on a computer it can become time-consuming to work your way through all of your near-identical shots. The Media Browser offers a useful solution to this by enabling the stacking of similar images, so that you can view a single thumbnail rather than several. To do this:

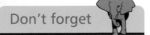

Beware

You can remove images from a stack by selecting the stack in the Media Browser and selecting Edit>Stack>Flatten Stack from the Menu bar. However, this will remove all of the images, apart from the top one, from the Media Browser. This does not remove them from your hard drive, although there is an option to do this too, if you wish.

1 Select the images that you want to stack in the Media Browser

2 Select Edit>Stack>Stack Selected Photos from the Menu bar

3 The images are stacked into a single thumbnail and the existence of the stack is indicated by this icon

Photo Stack

Don't forget

To revert stacked images to their original state, select Edit> Stack>Unstack Photos from the Menu bar.

4 To view all of the stacked images, click here

5 Click here to return to all of the photos in the Media Browser

Version Sets

When working with digital images it is commonplace to create several different versions from a single image. This could be to use one for printing and one for use on the Web, or because there are elements of an image that you want to edit. Instead of losing track of images that have been edited it is possible to create stacked thumbnails of edited images, which are known as version sets. These can include the original image and all of the edited versions. Version sets can be created and added to from either the Media Browser or the Editor. To do this:

1 Open an image

2 Make editing changes to the image in either Full Edit or Quick Fix mode

3 Select File>Save As from the Menu bar

4 Check on the Save in Version Set with Original box and click Save

5 A dialog box alerts you to the fact that the image has been edited but the original has not been altered. Click OK

6 The original image and the edited one are grouped together in a stack, and the fact that it is a version set is denoted underneath the set

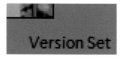

7 To view all of the images in a version set, select the set and select Edit>Version Set>Reveal Photos in Version Set from the Menu bar

Don't forget

The other version set menu options are Flatten Version Set, and Revert to Original. The latter deletes all of the other versions except the original image.

Tagging Images

As your digital image collection begins to grow on your computer it is increasingly important to be able to keep track of your images and find the ones you want, when you want them. One way of doing this is by assigning specific tags to images. You can then search for images according to the tags that have been added to them. The tagging function is accessed from the Task Pane within the Organizer. To add tags to images:

Don't forget

The Task Pane can also be accessed by selecting Window>Show Task Pane from the Organizer Menu bar.

1 If the Task Pane is not visible, select Window>Show Task Pane from the Menu Bar, or click here on the right border of the Media Browser to expand the Task Pane

2 Click here to access the currently available tags

3 Click here to access sub-categories for a particular category

Hot tip

When you create a new category you can also choose a new icon too.

4 Click here to add categories, or sub-categories, of your own choice

5 Enter a name for the new category, or sub-category, and click on the OK button

Create Sub-Category ✕

Sub-Category Name
Malawi

Parent Category or Sub-Category
Places ▼

OK   Cancel

6 Select the required images in the Media Browser

7 Drag a tag onto one of the selected images

▼ **Keyword Tags**

➕ ▾ ➖ 🖼 💡

▶ ☐ People
▼ ☐ Places
☐ Malawi

8 The images are tagged with the icon that denotes the main category, rather than the sub-category

▼ Keyword Tags
➕ ▾ ➖ 🖼 💡
▶ ☐ People
▼ ☐ Places
   ☐ **Malawi**
   ☐ York
☐ Events
☐ Other
▶ ☐ Imported Keyword Tags
▶ Smart Tags

★ ★ ★ ★ ★
12/12/2011

People Recognition

People shots are popular in most types of photography. However, this can result in hundreds, or thousands, of photos of different people. In Elements there is a feature that enables you to tag people throughout your collections. This is known as people recognition. To use this:

40

 In the Organizer, either select individual images, or do not select any to have people recognition applied to the whole collection

 Select Find>Find People for Tagging from the Menu bar

 The Organizer will analyze each photo and display a prompt box for each new face it finds

 Enter a name in the prompt box

 When the next face is identified, click on the arrow next to the name to access the face recognition confirmation box

6 Select matching faces in the Unconfirmed section of the People Recognition – Confirming window

Select images by clicking and dragging over them, or holding down the Ctrl button and clicking on specific images.

7 Click on the Save button and repeat Step 6, if prompted

8 Once all of the images have been identified with the required person a confirmation box appears. Click on the OK button

People Recognition really comes into its own when you have tagged dozens, or hundreds, of photos. You can then view all of the photos containing a specific person.

9 Check on the box next to a name to display the binoculars. All of the tagged images are displayed within the Organizer

Searching for Images

Once images have been tagged they can be searched for using both of these options. To do this:

 For tags and collections, click on this box so that the binoculars are showing, or

 Drag one of the icons below the timeline in the Media Browser

Hot tip

You can also search for items by using the Search box, located underneath the Menu bar. This can be used to search for images, video clips, audio clips, PDF files and projects.

 All matching items for a search are shown together within the Media Browser

 Click on the Show All button to return to the rest of the images

Multiple searches

Within the Media Browser, it is possible to search for images that have multiple (i.e. two or more) tags attached for them. For instance, you can search for images that have two named people tagged in them, without seeing all of the images in which the people are tagged individually. To do this:

 Tag images for one person

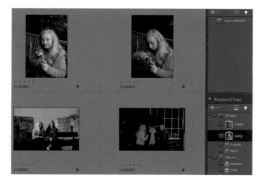

② Tag images for another person (make sure that at least one is the same as for the person in Step 1)

③ Check on the boxes next to the two people in the Keywords tag panel

④ Only the images that contain both of the tags are displayed

...cont'd

Searching by objects

In Elements 10 it is also possible to search for images based on specific objects. For instance, you can search for images with a particular building, landscape or animal. To do this:

1 Click on an image that contains the object which you want to use for the search criteria

2 Click on the down arrow next to the Search box in the Options bar in the Media Browser

Q Search

3 Select the Object Search option

Q Search
Text Search...

Try these new visual searches....
Visual Similarity Search
Object Search
Duplicate Photo Search

4 **D**rag the markers of the box over the object to resize it, or click and drag inside it to move the whole box

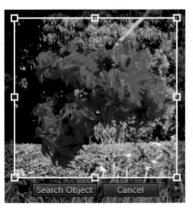

Search Object   Cancel

5   Click on the Search Object button   

6   Images with similar objects are displayed, with a percentage rating of how close the object match is

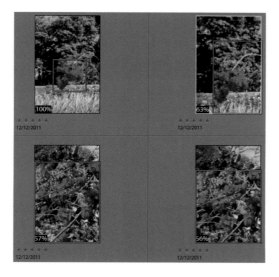

7   Drag this slider to refine the search according to Color or Shape

8   Click on the Options button and select Save Search Criteria As Smart Album to save the search

9   Enter a name for the Smart Album and click OK

Albums

Albums in Elements are similar to physical photo albums: they are a location into which you can store all your favorite groups of images. Once they have been stored there they can easily be found when required. To create albums:

1 In the Organizer, click on the Albums tab and select New Album

2 Enter a name for the new album and click Done

3 Select the images that you would like included in the new album and click on the Done button

4 The selected images are placed into the new album

5 Click here to view all of the images in a specific album

Date View

Date View is a function that offers the facility for viewing downloaded images in a calendar format. This can be viewed for either a year, a month or a day. The images are placed in the calendar according to the date on which they were taken, edited or downloaded. To use Date View:

1 In the Organizer, click here and select Date View

2 Click here to move through the calendar

3 Double-click on an image to view all of the items for that specific day in the full window

4 Select a day and click here to view all of the images for that day in a slide show

Hot tip

Click on the name of a month at the top of a calendar to see a list of available years. Those with an icon next to them contain photos.

47

5 Select an option here to view the calendar in Year, Month or Day format. Click on the Media Browser button to return to this view

Opening and Saving Images

Once you have captured images with a digital camera, or a scanner, and stored them on your computer, you can open them in Elements. There are a number of options for this:

Open command

1 Select File>Open from the Menu bar

2 Select an image from your hard drive and click Open

Open As command

This can be used to open a file in a different file format from its original format. To do this:

1 Select File>Open As from the Menu bar

2 Select an image and select the file format. Click Open

Saving images

When saving digital images, it is always a good idea to save them in at least two different file formats, particularly if layered objects, such as text and shapes, have been added. One of these formats should be the proprietary Photoshop format PSD or PDD. The reason for using this is that it will retain all of the layered information within an image. So, if a text layer has been added, it will still be available for editing, once it has been saved and closed.

The other format that an image should be saved in, is the one most appropriate for the use to which it is going to be put. Therefore, images that are going to be used on the Web should be saved as JPEG, GIF or PNG files, while an image that is going to be used for printing should be saved in another format, such as TIFF. Once images have been saved in these formats, all of the layered information within them becomes flattened into a single layer and it will not be possible to edit this once the image has been saved. By default, images are saved in the same format as the one in which they were opened.

Don't forget

Another option for opening files is the Open Recently Edited File command, which is accessed from the File menu. This lists, in order, the files you have opened most recently.

Don't forget

A proprietary file format is one that is specific to the program being used. It has greater flexibility when used within the program itself but cannot be distributed as easily as a JPEG or a GIF image.

Don't forget

The Save As command should be used if you want to make a copy of an image with a different file name. Editing changes can then be made to the copy, while the original remains untouched.

Working with Video

As well as using Elements for viewing and organizing photos, it can also be used in the same way with video. Video can be imported into Elements in a number of ways:

- From a camera that has video recording capabilities

- From a digital video camera

- From a cell/mobile phone

- From video that has been created in the Elements Premiere program. This is a companion program to Elements and is used to manipulate and edit video. It can be bought in a package with Elements, or individually. See www.adobe.com/products/premiereel/ for more details

To download video into Elements:

Don't forget

Elements Premiere can be bought as a package with Elements, or it can be bought individually.

1. Connect the device containing the video. Select the required device and download in the same way as for photos

Get Photos from:

NOKIA

2. The video is downloaded and displayed in the Organizer in the same way as photos

Beware

Video files are usually much larger in size than photos, and if you have many of them they will take up a lot of space on your computer.

3. Video clips are identified by this symbol

...cont'd

Viewing video

To view video clips:

 Double-click on the clip in the Organizer. The Elements video player will open and play the video clip

 Use the controls underneath the video window to navigate through the clip and adjust the volume

Don't forget

The Find>By Media Type option can also be used to find audio files, projects and PDFs.

Finding video

To find video clips within Elements:

In the Organizer, select Find>By Media Type>Video from the Menu bar

3 First Digital Steps

This chapter shows how to get up and running with digital image editing, and details some effective editing techniques for improving digital images, such as improving the overall color, removing unwanted items and changing the size and shape of images.

Color Enhancements

Some of the simplest, but most effective, editing changes that can be made to digital images are color enhancements. These can help to transform a mundane image into a stunning one, and Elements offers a variety of methods for achieving this. Some of these are verging towards the professional end of image editing, while others are done almost automatically by Elements. These are known as Auto adjustments and some simple manual adjustments can also be made to the brightness and contrast of an image. All of these color enhancement features can be accessed from the Enhance menu on the Menu bar.

Auto Levels

This automatically adjusts the overall color tone in an image in relation to the lightest and darkest points in the image:

Auto Contrast

This automatically adjusts the contrast in an image:

Auto Color Correction

This automatically adjusts all the color elements within an image:

Adjust Brightness/Contrast

This can be used to manually adjust the brightness and contrast in an image:

1   Select Enhance>Adjust Lighting>Brightness/Contrast from the Menu bar

2   Drag the sliders to adjust the image brightness and contrast

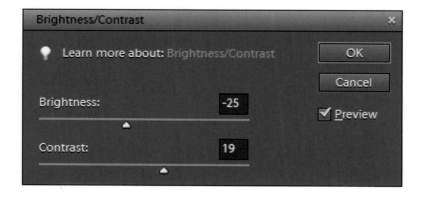

3   Click on the OK button

Don't forget

Apply small amounts of Brightness and Contrast at a time when you are editing an image. This will help ensure that the end result does not look too unnatural.

Hot tip

Always make sure that the Preview box is checked when you are applying color enhancements. This will display the changes as you make them and before they are applied to the image.

...cont'd

Adjust Shadows/Highlights

One problem that most photographers encounter at some point, is where part of an image is exposed correctly while another part is either over- or under-exposed. If this is corrected using general color correction techniques, such as levels or brightness and contrast, the poorly exposed area may be improved, but at the expense of the area that was correctly exposed initially. To overcome this, the Shadows/Highlights command can be used to adjust particular tonal areas of an image. To do this:

54

 Open an image where one part is correctly exposed and another part is incorrectly exposed

 Select Enhance> Adjust Lighting> Shadows/Highlights from the Menu bar

3 Make the required adjustments using the sliders or by entering figures in the boxes

4 Click OK

5 The poorly exposed areas of the image have been corrected, without altering the rest of the properly exposed image

Cropping

Cropping is a technique that can be used to remove unwanted areas of an image and highlight the main subject. The area to be cropped can only be selected as a rectangle. To crop an image:

 Select the Crop tool from the Toolbox

 Click and drag on an image to select the area to be cropped. The area that is selected is retained and the area to be cropped appears grayed-out

 Click and drag on these markers to resize the crop area

 Click on the check mark to accept the changes, or the circle to reject them

...cont'd

Overlay crop options

When performing cropping it is also possible to use various overlay grids to help the composition of the image. One of these is the Rule of Thirds. This is a photographic technique where a nine segment grid is used to position elements within the image. Generally, the items that you want to give the most prominence to should be positioned at one of the intersections of the lines. To use the Rule of Thirds grid:

 Select the Crop tool and from the Overlay options on the Options bar, select the Rule of Thirds option

 Crop the image so that at least one of the main subjects is located at the intersections of the lines in grid. This can be in the foreground or the background

The image is cropped according to the Rule of Thirds grid

Images can also be cropped using a larger grid. This can be useful if you are trying to align items within an image:

Another overlay option is the Golden Ratio. This is based on a complicated mathematical formula that is thought to create the most aesthetically pleasing ratio in terms of where a main subject appears. If the Golden Ratio overlay is used, the main subject should appear at the point of the dot in the overlay:

Don't forget

The different grid options are all accessed from the Overlay box on the Options bar.

Don't forget

Although the Golden Ratio is a mathematical equation based on the ratio of quantities, it has been adopted by artists and architects for hundreds of years due to its perceived aesthetic qualities and appeal.

57

Cloning

Cloning is a technique that can be used to copy one area of an image over another. This can be used to cover up small imperfections in an image, such as a dust mark or a spot, and also to copy or remove large items in an image, such as a person.

To clone items:

1 Select the Clone Stamp tool from the Toolbox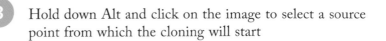

2 Set the Clone Stamp options in the Options bar

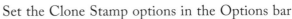

3 Hold down Alt and click on the image to select a source point from which the cloning will start

4 Drag the cursor to copy everything over which the selection point marker passes

Pattern Cloning

The Pattern Stamp tool can be used to copy a selected pattern over an image, or a selected area of an image. To do this:

1 Select the Pattern Stamp tool from the Toolbox

2 Click here in the Options bar to select a pattern

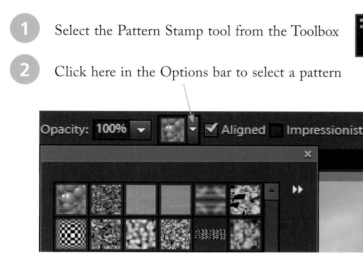

3 Click and drag on an image to copy the selected pattern over it

Don't forget

The Pattern Stamp tool is grouped in the Toolbox with the Clone Stamp tool. It can be selected from the Options bar, or by clicking and holding on the black triangle in the corner of the Clone Stamp tool and then selecting the Pattern Stamp tool from the subsequent list.

Hot tip

Patterns can be added to the patterns panel by selecting an image, or an area of an image, and selecting Edit> Define Pattern from the Editor Menu bar. Then give the pattern a name in the Pattern Name dialog box and click OK.

Healing Brush

One of the favorite techniques in digital imaging is removing unwanted items, particularly physical blemishes, such as spots and wrinkles. This can be done with the Clone tool but the effects can sometimes be too harsh, as a single area is copied over the affected item. A more subtle effect can be achieved with the Healing Brush and the Spot Healing Brush tools. The Healing Brush can be used to remove blemishes over larger areas, such as wrinkles:

1 Open an image with blemishes covering a reasonably large area, i.e. more than a single spot

2 Select the Healing Brush tool from the Toolbox and make the required selections in the Options bar

Brush: 19   Mode: Normal

3 Hold down Alt and click on an area of the image to load the Healing Brush tool. Drag over the affected area. The cross is the area which is copied beneath the circle. At this point the overall tone is not perfect and looks too pink

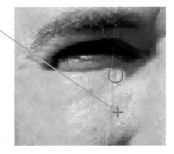

4 Release the mouse and the Healing Brush blends the affected area with the one that was copied over it. This creates a much more natural skin tone

Spot Healing Brush

The Spot Healing Brush is very effective for quickly removing small blemishes in an image, such as spots. To do this:

 1 Open an image and zoom in on the area with the blemish

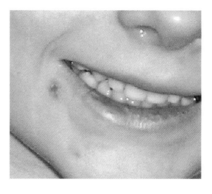

2 Select the Spot Healing Brush tool from the Toolbox and make the required selections in the Options bar

Size: **13 px**

3 Drag the Spot Healing Brush tool over the affected area

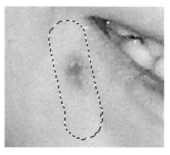

4 The blemish is removed and the overall skin tone is retained

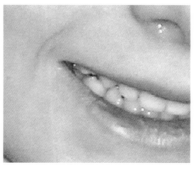

Uncluttering a Photo

As well as using the healing brushes for removing small blemishes, the Healing Brush tool can also be used to remove larger objects in the foreground or background of an image. This can be a very effective way to unclutter a photo. To do this:

1 Open the image with the objects that you want to remove

2 Select the Healing Brush tool

3 Select the brush size for the Healing Brush. This can be quite large if it is a fairly uniformed area that will be copied

4 Hold down Alt and click on an area that you want to use to copy

over the object you want to remove

5 Drag the Healing Brush tool over the objects you want to remove. This will then be blended with the area selected in Step 4

6 The unwanted object(s) are removed from the photo. This is effective for either the foreground or the background of the photo. In some cases the Healing Brush tool may need to be loaded from different locations to blend the different areas of the photo as accurately as possible

Rotating

Various rotation commands can be applied to images, and also individual layers in layered images. This can be useful for positioning items and also for correcting the orientation of an image that is on its side or upside down.

Rotating a whole image

1 Select Image>Rotate from the Menu bar

2 Select a rotation option from the menu

3 Select Custom to enter your own value for the amount you want an image rotated

	90° Left
	90° Right
	180°
	Custom...
	Flip Horizontal
	Flip Vertical
	Free Rotate Layer
	Layer 90° Left
	Layer 90° Right
	Layer 180°
	Flip Layer Horizontal
	Flip Layer Vertical
	Straighten and Crop Image
	Straighten Image

Rotate Canvas

Angle: **3**   ○ °Right   ○ °Left   OK   Cancel

4 Click on the OK button   OK

Rotating a layer

To rotate separate layers within an image:

Don't forget

For more information about working with layers, see Chapter Seven.

1 Open an image that consists of two or more layers. Select one of the layers in the Layers panel

2 Select Image>Rotate from the Menu bar

3 Select a layer rotation option from the menu

4 The selected layer is rotated independently

Transforming

The Transform commands can be used to resize an image, and to apply some basic distortion techniques. These commands can be accessed by selecting Image>Transform from the Menu bar.

Free Transform

This enables you to manually alter the size and shape of an image. To do this:

 1 Select Image>Transform>Free Transform from the Menu bar

2 Click and drag here to transform the vertical and horizontal size of the image. Hold down Shift to transform it in proportion

Don't forget

The other options from the Transform menu are Skew, Distort and Perspective. These can be accessed and applied in a similar way to the Free Transform option.

65

Magnification

There are a number of ways in Elements in which the magnification at which an image is being viewed can be increased or decreased. This can be useful if you want to zoom in on a particular part of an image, for editing purposes, or if you want to view a whole image to see the result of editing effects that have been applied.

View menu

 Select View from the Menu bar and select one of the options from the View menu

Zoom tool

 Select the Zoom tool from the Toolbox

Click once on an image to enlarge it (usually by 100% each time). Hold down Alt and click to decrease the magnification

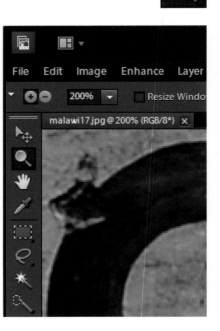

Navigator panel

This can be used to move around an image and also magnify certain areas. To use the Navigator panel:

1 Access the Navigator panel by selecting Window>Navigator from the Menu bar

2 Drag this slider to magnify the area of the image within the red rectangle

3 Drag the rectangle to change the area of the image that is being magnified

Eraser

The Eraser tool can be used to remove areas of an image. In a simple, single layer image, this can just leave a blank hole, which has to be filled with something. The Eraser options are:

1 Eraser, which can be used to erase part of the background image or a layer within it

2 Background Eraser, which can be used to remove an uneven background

3 Magic Eraser, which can be used to quickly remove a solid background (see below)

Erasing a background

With the Magic Eraser tool, it is possible to delete a colored background in an image. To do this:

1 Open an image with an evenly colored background

2 Select the Magic Eraser and make the required selections in the Options bar. Make sure the Contiguous box is not checked

3 Click once on the background. It is removed from the image, regardless of where it occurs

④ Quick Wins

This chapter looks at some of these "quick wins" that can be done in Elements and also shows some of the Guided Edit functions that can be used to achieve a variety of stunning photo effects.

Removing Red-eye

One of the most common problems with photographs of people, whether they are taken digitally or with a film-based camera, is red-eye. This is caused when the camera's flash is used and then reflects in the subject's pupils. This can create the dreaded red-eye effect, when the subject can unintentionally be transformed into a demonic character. Unless you have access to professional studio lighting equipment, or have a removable flash unit that can be positioned away from the subject's face, sooner or later you will capture images that contain red-eye.

Elements has recognized that removing red-eye is one of the top priorities for most amateur photographers and a specific tool for this purpose has been included in the Toolbox: the Red Eye Removal tool. To use this:

Hot tip

The best way to deal with red-eye is to avoid it in the first place. Try using a camera that has a red-eye reduction function. This uses an extra flash, just before the picture is taken, to diminish the effect of red-eye.

 1   Open an image that contains red-eye

2   Select the Zoom tool from the Toolbox

3 Drag around the affected area until it appears at a suitable magnification

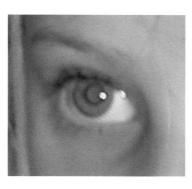

Hot tip

Red-eye can be removed by clicking near the affected area: it does not have to be directly on it.

4 Select the Red Eye Removal tool from the Toolbox

5 Click in the Options bar to select the

size of the pupil and the amount by which it will be darkened

6 Click once on the red-eye, or drag around the affected area

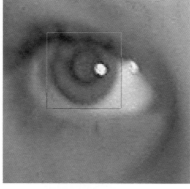

Hot tip

Red-eye can also be removed when images are being downloaded from the camera. This is an option in the Photo Downloader window.

7 The red-eye is removed

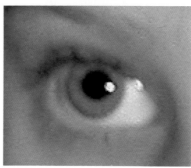

Changing to Black and White

Most digital cameras and scanners are capable of converting color images into black and white at the point of capture. However, it is also possible to use Elements to convert existing color images into black and white ones. To do this:

1 Open a color image and select Enhance>Convert to Black and White from the Menu bar

2 The Convert to Black and White dialog box has various options for how the image is converted

3 Select the type of black and white effect to be applied, depending on the subject in the image

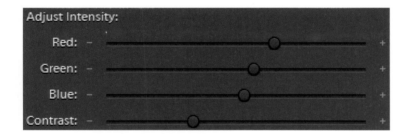

Select a style:

- Infrared Effect
- Newspaper
- Portraits
- **Scenic Landscape**
- Urban/Snapshots
- Vivid Landscapes

4 Drag these sliders to specify the intensity of the effect to be applied for different elements

Adjust Intensity:

Red:	– ⎯⎯⎯⎯⎯◯⎯⎯⎯⎯ +
Green:	– ⎯⎯⎯⎯◯⎯⎯⎯⎯⎯ +
Blue:	– ⎯⎯⎯◯⎯⎯⎯⎯⎯⎯ +
Contrast:	– ⎯⎯◯⎯⎯⎯⎯⎯⎯⎯ +

5 Click on the OK button

OK

6 The image is converted into black and white, according to the settings that have been selected

Hot tip

A similar effect can be achieved by selecting Enhance>Adjust Color>Remove Color from the Menu bar.

Adjusting Skin Tones

Skin tone can sometimes cause problems in digital images. At times they can look washed-out and pale or contain a slightly unnatural color cast. This can be edited with the Adjust Skin Tones function, which can be used to improve the skin tone of a pale image, or just to give someone a more tanned or healthy appearance. To do this:

Beware

It is best to make small adjustments when editing skin tones, otherwise the results can look too unnatural.

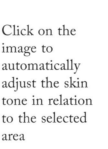 In the Editor, open an image whose skin tone you want to adjust

2 Select Enhance> Adjust Color> Adjust Color for Skin Tone from the Menu bar

3 Click on the image to automatically adjust the skin tone in relation to the selected area

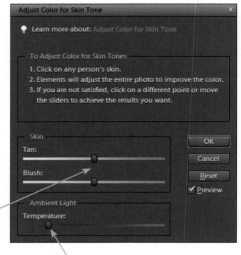

4 Drag these sliders to alter the amount of tan and blush in the skin tone

5 Drag this slider to edit the overall light in the image

6 Click on the OK button

Quick Edit Options

The Quick Edit options in Elements offer a number of functions within the one location. This makes it easier to apply a number of techniques at the same time.

Using Quick Edit

 1 Open an image in the Editor and click on the Edit Quick button

2 Click here for options on how the image is displayed on screen

3 Click here for options for zooming, moving around the image and cropping

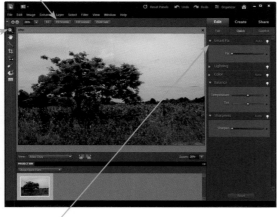

4 Correction panels are located here. Click a right-pointing arrow to expand a panel

5 Click here to specify how the editing changes are displayed

Hot tip

Several options can be applied sequentially, without having to leave the Quick Edit window. To do this, click the check mark in each panel after each effect has been selected.

75

...cont'd

Smart Fix

This performs several editing changes in a single operation. Click on the Auto button to have the changes applied automatically, or drag the slider to specify the amount of the editing changes.

Lighting Fixes

This provides options for adjusting the lighting and contrast in an image. Click on the Auto buttons to adjust the lighting range within an image and the contrast. Drag the sliders to adjust the lightest, darkest and midtone areas within an image.

Don't forget

Changes are displayed in the main Quick Fix window as they are being made.

Don't forget

In general, when applying lighting fixes, it is more effective to apply them manually rather than using the Auto functions.

Color Fixes

Click on the Auto button to adjust the hue and saturation in an image, or drag the sliders to make manual adjustments.

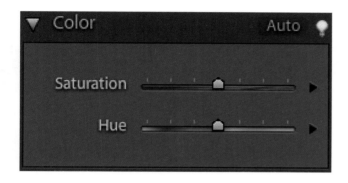

Balance Fixes

Drag the sliders to adjust the warmth of the colors in an image and the color balance.

Sharpening Fixes

This can be used to apply sharpening to an image to make it clearer, either automatically with the Auto button or manually with the slider.

Working with Guided Edits

In Elements 10 the Guided Edit function has been enhanced to make it easier to perform both simple editing functions and also more complex image editing processes that consist of a number of steps. To use the various functions of Guided Edit:

 Open an image. Under the Edit tab, click on the Guided button

Edit	Create	Share
Full	Quick	Guided

In the Basic Photo Edits section, select a function such as Crop Photo

▼ Basic Edits

Crop Photo ›
Rotate and/or Straighten Photo ›
Sharpen Photo ›

Details about the selected function are displayed. Click on the tool that is displayed

Crop

A crop box has been drawn on your photo using the Crop tool. Resize the box to crop your photo to the desired size.

🗗 *Crop Tool*

To constrain the photo to a certain size or ratio, use the menu below.

Crop Box Size: No Restriction ▼

Overlay: Rule of Thirds ▼

The selected function is applied to the image. This can usually be edited once it has been applied

Hot tip

Guided Edits are a great way to become familiar with image editing and a lot of your needs will be catered for here. However, once you become confident with this you may want to expand your horizons and work with some more techniques in Full Edit mode.

5 In addition to one-step Guided Edits there are also more in-depth operations such as the Guide for Editing a Photo

6 This contains a number of steps that can be followed to improve a photo. The relevant tools are available for each step

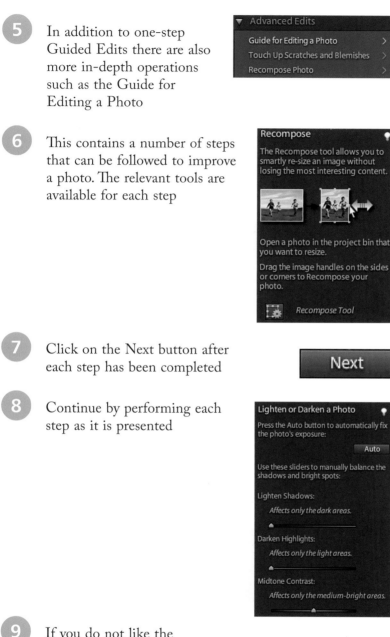

7 Click on the Next button after each step has been completed

8 Continue by performing each step as it is presented

9 If you do not like the appearance of the photo click on the Reset button to return to its original state

10 Click on the Done button to complete the Guided Edit

Matching Photo Styles

Within the Guided Edits there are a number of Photomerge functions for creating a variety of special effects. (These can also be accessed from the Menu bar in Full Edit mode.) One of the Photomerge effects is for matching photo styles. This can be used when you want to apply the style from one photo to another:

 Open an image. Under the Edit tab, click on the Guided button

Edit	Create	Share
Full	Quick	Guided

80

 In the Photomerge section click on the Style Match button

▼ Photomerge	
Group Shot	>
Faces	>
Scene Cleaner	>
Exposure	>
Style Match	>

3 The image is opened in the Style Match window. The source image appears in the right-hand panel

Photo styles appear in the Style Bin, which is located next to the Project Bin

 Drag a photo style into the left-hand panel. The style is applied to the source image on the right

81

 The photo style can be edited within the Style Match panel by dragging these sliders

Touch Up Quick Edits

Touch Up Quick Edits provide options for performing tasks, such as whitening teeth and brightening dull skies. To access the Touch Up Quick Edits, click here in the Quick Edit panel.

Brightening dull skies
To make dull skies appear brighter:

The Make Dull Skies Blue tool applies the effect to everything in the selection. This can result in clouds taking on a bluish tinge.

 Open an image with a sky you want to brighten

 Click on the Make Dull Skies Blue tool

Drag the tool over the area of the sky you want to brighten. As you drag, the area will become selected and automatically brightened

Whitening teeth

Everyone likes to see white teeth in a photo, and with the teeth whitening tool this is possible for anyone. To do this:

1 Open an image and click on the Whiten Teeth tool

2 Click on the Zoom tool

3 Drag the Zoom tool around the teeth area

4 Click here to select a brush size for the Whiten Teeth tool

5 Drag the Whiten Teeth tool over the teeth

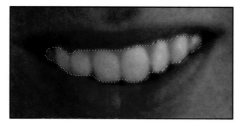

6 The teeth area is selected and whitened in one operation

Panoramas

Creating panoramas

For anyone who takes landscape pictures, the desire to create a panorama occurs sooner or later. With film-based cameras, this usually involves sticking several photographs together to create the panorama, albeit a rather patchwork one. With digital images the end result can look a lot more professional and Elements has a dedicated function for achieving this: Photomerge.

When creating a panorama there are a few rules to follow:

- If possible, use a tripod to ensure that your camera stays at the same level for all of the shots

- Keep the same exposure settings for all images

- Make sure that there is a reasonable overlap between images (about 20%). Some cameras enable you to align the correct overlap between the images

- Keep the same distance between yourself and the object you are capturing. Otherwise the end result will look out of perspective

To create a panorama:

Beware

Do not include too many images in a panorama, otherwise it could be too large for viewing or printing easily.

1. Select File>New>Photomerge Panorama from the Menu bar (or access from the Guided Edit section)

2. Select an option for the type of panorama image that you want to create

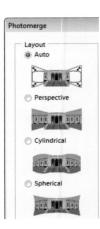

3 Click on the Browse button to locate images you want to use on your computer

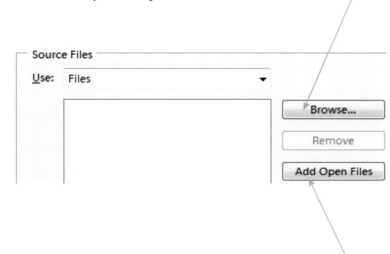

4 Or, click on the Add Open Files button to use images that are already open

5 If you Browse for images, select them from your computer

6 Click on the OK button

...cont'd

7 In some instances the final image may need some additional editing. One common problem is the appearance of diagonal lines across the image, particularly in the sky region

8 Panoramas can usually be improved by applying color correction such as Brightness/Contrast and Shadows/Highlights. They can also be cropped to straighten the borders

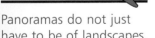
9 An unwanted line in a panorama can be removed by cloning from a nearby area, or by selecting it and applying color correction until it is the same tone as the rest of the image. Some trial and error may be needed to achieve exactly the right look

5 Beyond the Basics

Since Elements is based on the full version of Photoshop, it contains a number of powerful features for image editing. This chapter looks at some of these features and how to use them.

Hue and Saturation

The hue and saturation command can be used to edit the color elements of an image. However, it works slightly differently from other commands, such as those for the brightness and contrast. There are three areas that are covered by the hue and saturation command: color, color strength and lightness. To adjust the hue and saturation of an image:

 Open an image

Select Enhance> Adjust Color>Adjust Hue/Saturation

 Drag this slider to adjust the hue of the image, i.e. change the colors in the image

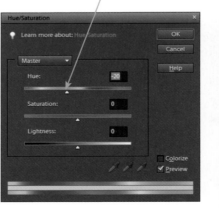

4 Drag this slider to adjust the saturation, i.e. the intensity of colors in the image

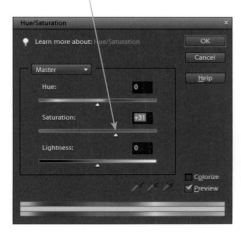

Don't forget

The Lightness option is similar to adjusting image brightness.

5 Check on the Colorize box to color the image with the hue of the currently selected foreground color in the Color Picker, which is located at the bottom of the Toolbox

Hot tip

The Colorize option can be used to create some interesting "color wash" effects. Try altering the Hue slider once the Colorize box has been checked on.

89

Don't forget

For more on working with color and the Color Picker, see Chapter Eight.

6 Click on the OK button to apply any changes that have been made

Histogram

The histogram is a device that displays the tonal range of the pixels in an image, and it can be used for very precise editing of an image. The histogram (Window>Histogram) is depicted in a graph format and it displays how the pixels in an image are distributed across the image, from the darkest (black) to the lightest (white) points. Another way of considering the histogram is that it displays the values of an image's highlights, midtones and shadows:

Don't forget

The histogram works by looking at the individual color channels of an image (Red, Green, Blue, also known as the RGB color model) or at a combination of all three, which is displayed as the Luminosity in the Channel box. It can also look at all of the colors in an image.

Highlights

Midtones

Shadows

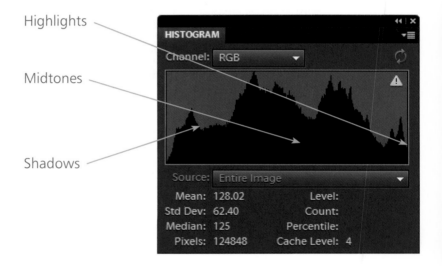

Don't forget

Image formats, such as JPEG, are edited in Elements using the RGB color model, i.e. red, green and blue mixed together to create the colors in the image.

Highlights

Midtones

Shadows

Ideally, the histogram graph should show a reasonably consistent range of tonal distribution, indicating an image that has good contrast and detail:

However, if the tonal range is bunched at one end of the graph, this indicates that the image is under-exposed or over-exposed:

If the histogram is left open, it will update automatically as editing changes are made to an image. This gives a good idea of how effective the changes are.

Over-exposure

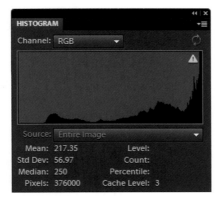

Under-exposure

Levels

While the histogram displays the tonal range of an image, the Levels function can be used to edit this range. Any changes made using the Levels function will then be visible in the histogram. Levels allow you to redistribute pixels between the darkest and lightest points in an image, and also to set these points manually if you want to. To use the Levels function:

Hot tip

The Levels function can be used to adjust the tonal range of a specific area of an image, by first making a selection and then using the Levels dialog box. For more details on selecting areas see Chapter Six.

1 Open an image

Don't forget

In the Levels dialog box, the graph is the same as the one shown in the histogram.

2 Select Enhance>Adjust Lighting>Levels from the Menu bar

Midtone input point

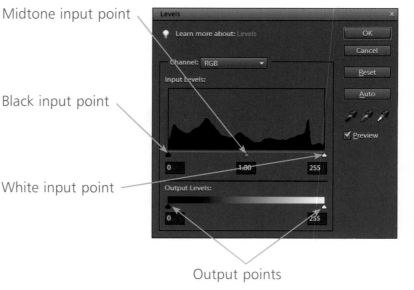

Black input point

Don't forget

Image shadows, midtones and highlights can be altered by dragging the markers for the black, midtone and white input points.

White input point

Output points

3 Drag the black point and the white point sliders to, or beyond, the first pixels denoted in the graph to increase the contrast

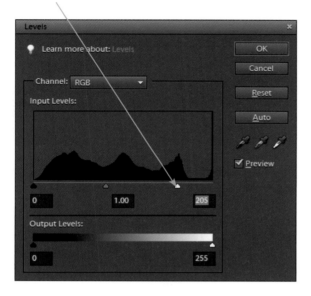

Don't forget

It is worth adjusting an image's black and white points before any other editing is performed.

4 Drag the output sliders towards the middle to decrease the contrast

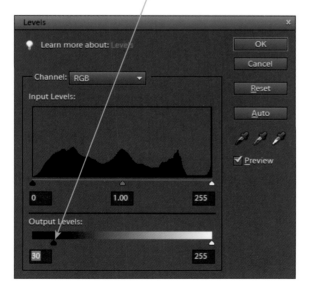

Hot tip

Move the midtones point slider to darken or lighten the midtones in an image.

Don't forget

The Auto button, in the Levels dialog box, produces the same effect as using the Enhance>Auto Levels command from the Menu bar.

Filter Adjustments

There are numerous special effects within the Content and Effects panels. However, there are also some filter effects that can be used to alter the color in the image. These are known as filter adjustment effects. To use these:

 Open an image and select Filter>Adjustments from the Menu bar

 Select either Equalize, Invert or Posterize

Equalize

Invert

Posterize

Unsharp Mask

Although sharpening is a useful technique for improving the overall definition of an image, it can sometimes appear too harsh and "jaggy". For a more subtle effect, the Unsharp Mask can be used. This works by increasing the contrast between light and dark pixels in an image. To use the Unsharp Mask:

 Open an image that you want to sharpen

Select the Enhance> Unsharp Mask option from the Menu bar

Apply the appropriate settings in the Unsharp Mask dialog box and click on the OK button

Don't forget

The settings for the Unsharp Mask are: Amount, which determines the amount to increase the contrast between pixels; Radius, which determines how many pixels will have the sharpening applied to them in an affected area; Threshold, which determines how different a pixel has to be from its neighbor before sharpening is applied.

 The contrast between light and dark pixels is increased, giving the impression of a clearer, or sharper, image

Importing RAW Images

RAW images are those in which the digital data has not been processed in any way, or converted into any specific file format, by the camera when they were captured. These produce high quality images and are usually available on higher specification digital cameras. However, RAW is becoming more common in consumer digital cameras and they can be downloaded in Elements in the same way as any other image. Once the RAW images are accessed, the Camera Raw dialog box opens so that a variety of editing functions can be applied to the image. RAW images act as a digital negative and have to be saved into another format before they can be used in the conventional way. To edit RAW images:

Beware

RAW images are much larger in file size than the same versions captured as JPEGs.

Don't forget

The RAW format should be used if you want to make manual changes to an image to achieve the highest possible quality.

1. Open a RAW image in the Editor or from the Organizer

2. In the Camera RAW dialog box, editing functions that are usually performed when an image is captured, can be made manually

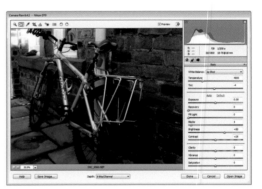

3. Click here to adjust the White Balance in the image

4. Drag these sliders to adjust the Color Temperature and Tint in the image

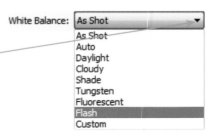

5 Drag these sliders to adjust the Exposure, Shadows, Brightness, Contrast and Saturation in the image

Auto   Default

Exposure	0.00
Recovery	0
Fill Light	0
Blacks	5
Brightness	+50
Contrast	+25

6 Click on the Detail tab and drag these sliders to adjust the Sharpness and Noise in the image

Detail

Sharpening

Amount	25
Radius	1.0
Detail	25
Masking	0

Noise Reduction

Luminance	0
Color	25

7 Click on the Open Image button. This opens the image in Full Edit mode, from where it can also be saved as a standard file format, such as JPEG

Open Image

Image Size

The physical size of a digital image can sometimes be a confusing issue, as it is frequently dealt with under the term "resolution". Unfortunately, resolution can be applied to a number of areas of digital imaging: image resolution, monitor resolution, print size and print resolution.

Image resolution

The resolution of an image is determined by the number of pixels in it. This is counted as a vertical and a horizontal value, e.g. 4000 x 3000. When multiplied together it gives the overall resolution, i.e. 12,000,000 pixels in this case. This is frequently the headline figure quoted by the manufacturers, e.g. 12 million pixels (or 12 megapixels). To view the image resolution in Elements:

1 Select Image> Resize>Image Size from the Menu bar

2 The image size is displayed here (in pixels)

Monitor resolution

Most modern computer monitors display digital images at between 72 and 96 pixels per inch (ppi). This means that every inch of the screen contains approximately this number of pixels. So, for an image being displayed at 100%, the onscreen size will be the number of pixels horizontally divided by 72 (or 96 depending on the monitor) and the same vertically. In the above example, this would mean the image would be viewed at 34 inches by 45 inches approximately (2448/72 and 3264/72) on a monitor. In modern web browsers this is usually adjusted so that the whole image is accommodated on the viewable screen.

Document size (print resolution)

Pixels in an image are not a set size, which means that images can be printed in a variety of sizes, simply by contracting or expanding the available pixels. This is done by changing the resolution in the Document Size section of the Image Size dialog box. (When dealing with document size, think of this as the size of the printed document.) To set the size at which an image will be printed:

Hot tip

The higher the print resolution, the better the final printed image. Aim for a minimum of 200 pixels per inch for the best printed output.

1 Select Image>Resize>Image Size from the Menu bar

2 Change the resolution here (or change the Width and Height of the document size). Make sure the Resample Image box is not checked

Hot tip

To work out the size at which an image will be printed, divide the pixel dimensions (height and width) by the resolution value under the Document Size heading.

66

Don't forget

The print resolution determines how many pixels are used in each inch of the printed image (ppi). However, the number of colored dots used to represent each pixel on the paper is determined by the printer resolution, measured in dots per inch (dpi). So if the print resolution is 72 ppi and the printer resolution is 2880 dpi, each pixel will be represented by 40 colored dots, i.e. 2880 divided by 72.

3 By changing one value, the other two are updated too. Click on the OK button

OK

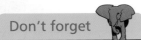

Don't forget

The process of adding pixels to an image to increase its size is known as "interpolation".

Beware

Since it involves digital guesswork by Elements, resampling up results in inferior image quality.

Hot tip

To keep the same resolution for an image, resample it by changing the pixel dimensions' height and width. To keep the same Document Size (i.e. the size at which it will be printed) resample it by changing the resolution.

Beware

Make sure the Constrain Proportions box is checked on if you want the image to be increased or decreased in size proportionally, rather than just one value being altered independently of the other.

Resampling Images

All digital images can be increased or decreased in size. This involves adding or removing pixels from the image. Decreasing the size of an image is relatively straightforward and involves removing redundant pixels. However, increasing the size of an image involves adding pixels by digital guesswork. To do this, Elements looks at the existing pixels and works out the nearest match for the ones that are to be added. Increasing or decreasing the size of a digital image is known as "resampling".

Resampling

Resampling down decreases the size of the image and it is more effective than resampling up. To do this:

1. Select Image> Resize>Image Size from the Menu bar

2. Check the Resample Image box

3. Resample the image by changing the pixel dimensions, the height and width or the resolution

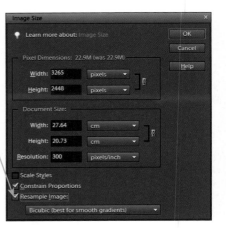

4. Changing any of the values above alters the physical size of the image. Click on the OK button

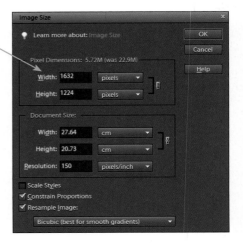

6 Selecting Areas

The true power of digital image editing comes into its own when you are able to select areas of an image and edit them independently. This chapter looks at the various ways that selections can be made and edited within Elements.

About Selections

One of the most important aspects of image editing is the ability to select areas within an image. This can be used in a number of different ways:

- Selecting an object to apply an editing technique to it (such as changing the brightness or contrast) without affecting the rest of the image

- Selecting a particular color in an image

- Selecting an area to apply a special effect to it

- Selecting an area to remove it

Elements has several tools that can be used to select items, and there are also a number of editing functions that can be applied to selections.

Two examples of how selections can be used are:

 Select an area within an image and delete it

 Select an area and add a color or special effect

Don't forget

Once a selection has been made it stays selected, even when another tool is activated, to allow for editing to take place.

Hot tip

The best way to deselect a selection is to click on it once with one of the selection tools, preferably the one used to make the selection.

Marquee Tools

There are two options for the Marquee tool: the Rectangular Marquee tool and the Elliptical Marquee tool. Both of these can be used to make symmetrical selections. To use the Marquee tools:

1 Select either the Rectangular or the Elliptical Marquee tool from the Toolbox. Select the required options from the Options bar

2 Make a symmetrical selection with one of the tools by clicking and dragging on an image

Don't forget

To access additional tools from the Toolbox, click and hold on the black triangle next to one of the default tools, and select one of the subsequent options that are available.

Elliptical selection   Rectangular selection

Hot tip

To make a selection that is exactly square or round, hold down Shift when dragging with the Rectangular Marquee tool or the Elliptical Marquee tool respectively.

Lasso Tools

There are three options for the Lasso tools, which can be used to make freehand selections. To use these:

Lasso tool

1 Select the Lasso tool from the Toolbox and select the required options from the Options bar

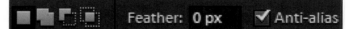

2 Make a freehand selection by clicking and dragging around an object

Polygonal Lasso tool

1 Select the Polygonal Lasso tool from the Toolbox and select the required options from the Options bar

2 Make a selection by clicking on specific points around an object, and then dragging to the next point

Magnetic Lasso tool

1 Select the Magnetic Lasso tool from the Toolbox and select the required options from the Options bar

2 Click once on an image to create the first anchor point

On the Options bar for the Magnetic Lasso tool, the Edge Contrast value determines the amount of contrast there has to be between colors for the selection line to snap to them. A high value detects lines with a high contrast and vice versa.

3 Make a selection by dragging continuously around an object. The selection line snaps to the closest strongest edge, i.e. the one with the most contrast. Fastening points are added as the selection is made

Don't forget

The Frequency setting on the Options bar determines how quickly the fastening points are inserted as a selection is being made. A high value places the fastening points more quickly than a low value.

Magic Wand Tool

The Magic Wand tool can be used to select areas of the same, or similar, color. To do this:

Don't forget

On the Options bar for the Magic Wand tool, the Tolerance box determines the range of colors that will be selected in relation to the color you click on. A low value will only select a very narrow range of colors in relation to the initially selected one, while a high value will include a greater range. The values range from 0–255.

Hot tip

On the Options bar for the Magic Wand tool, check on the Contiguous box to ensure that only adjacent colors are selected. To select the same, or similar, color throughout the image, whether adjacent or not, uncheck the Contiguous box so that there is no tick showing.

1 Select the Magic Wand tool from the Toolbox and select the required options from the Options bar

Tolerance: 32 ✔ Anti-alias ✔ Contiguous ☐ Sample All Layers

2 Click on a color to select all of the adjacent pixels that are the same, or similar, color, depending on the options selected from the Options bar

Selection Brush Tool

The Selection Brush tool can be used to select areas by using a brush-like stroke. Unlike with the Marquee or Lasso tools, the area selected by the Selection Brush tool is the one directly below where the tool moves. To make a selection with the Selection Brush tool:

 Select the Selection Brush tool from the Toolbox and select the required options from the Options bar

Don't forget

The Selection Brush tool can be used to select an area, or to mask an area. This can be determined in the Mode box in the Options bar.

Click and drag to make a selection

The selection area is underneath the borders of the Selection Brush tool

Quick Selection Tool

The Quick Selection tool can be used to select areas of similar color by drawing over the general area, without having to make a specific selection. To do this:

1 Select the Quick Selection tool from the Toolbox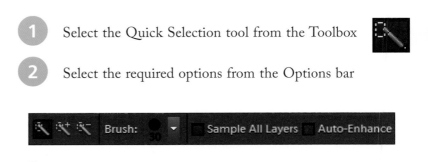

2 Select the required options from the Options bar

3 Draw over an area, or part of an area, to select all of the similarly colored pixels

Smart Brush Tool

The Smart Brush tool can be used to quickly select large areas in an image (in a similar way to the Quick Selection tool) and then have effects applied automatically to the selected area. To do this:

1. Open the image to which you want to apply changes with the Smart Brush tool

Don't forget

Multiple editing effects can be applied with the Smart Brush tool within the same image. This usually requires selecting different parts of the image and selecting the required effect.

2. Select the Smart Brush tool from the Toolbox

3. Select the editing effect you want to apply to the area selected by the Smart Brush tool, from the Options bar

4. Select Brush size for the Smart Brush tool, from the Options bar

5. Drag the Smart Brush tool over an area of the image. In the left-hand image, below, the building has been selected and brightened, in the right-hand image the sky has been selected and enhanced

Don't forget

For more information about adding effects with the Smart Brush tool, see Chapter Nine.

Inverting a Selection

This can be a useful option if you have edited a selection and then want to edit the rest of the image without affecting the area you have just selected. To do this:

 Make a selection

 Choose Select> Inverse from the Menu bar

 The selection becomes inverted, i.e. if a background object was selected the foreground is now selected

Feathering

Feathering is a technique that can be used to soften the edges of a selection by making them slightly blurry. This can be used if you are pasting a selection into another image, or if you want to soften the edges around a portrait of an individual. To do this:

 Make a selection

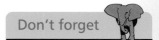

Don't forget

Feathering can also be selected from the Options bar once a Marquee tool is selected, and before the selection has been made.

Choose Select> Feather from the Menu bar

Enter a Feather value (the number of pixels around the radius of the selection

that will be blurred). Click on the OK button

Hot tip

If required, crop the final image so that the feathered subject is more prominent.

Invert the selection, as shown on the previous page, and delete the background by pressing Delete. This will leave the selection around the subject with softened edges

111

Editing Selections

When you have made a selection, you can edit it in a number of ways.

Moving a selection
Make a selection and select the Move tool from the Toolbox. Drag the selection to move it to a new location.

Changing the selection area
Make a selection with a selection tool. With the same tool selected, click and drag within the selection area to move it over another part of the image.

Adding to a selection
Make a selection and click on this button in the Options bar. Make another selection to create a single larger selection. The two selections do not have to intersect.

Intersecting with a selection
To create a selection by intersecting two existing selections: make a selection and click on this button in the Options bar. Make another selection that intersects the first. The intersected area will become the selection.

Expanding a selection
To expand a selection by a specific number of pixels: make a selection and choose Select>Modify>Expand from the Menu bar. In the Expand Selection dialog box, enter the amount by which you want the selection expanded.

Growing a selection
The Grow command can be used on a selection when it has been made with the Magic Wand tool, and some of the pixels within the selection have been omitted. To do this:

Make a selection with the Magic Wand tool and make the required choices from the Options bar. Choose Select>Grow from the Menu bar. Depending on the choices in the Options bar, the omitted pixels will be included in the selection.

Beware

Once an area has been moved and deselected, it cannot then be selected independently again, unless it has been copied and pasted onto a separate layer.

Don't forget

To deselect a selection, click once inside the selection area with the tool that was used to make the selection.

7 Layers

Layers provide the means to add numerous elements to an image, and edit them independently from one another. This chapter looks at how to use layers to expand your creative possibilities.

Layering Images

Layering is a technique that enables you to add additional elements to an image, and place them on separate layers, so that they can be edited and manipulated independently from other elements in the image. It is like creating an image using transparent sheets of film: each layer is independent of the others but, when they are combined, a composite image is created. This is an extremely versatile technique for working with digital images.

By using layers, several different elements can be combined to create a composite image:

Original image

Final image
With text and a shape added (two additional layers have been added).

Layers Panel

The use of layers within Elements is governed by the Layers panel. When an image is first opened it is shown in the Layers panel as the Background layer. While this remains as the Background layer it cannot be moved above any other layers. However, it can be converted into a normal layer, in which case it operates in the same way as any other layer. To convert a Background layer into a normal one:

1 The open image is shown in the Layers panel as the Background

2 Double-click here

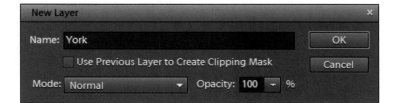

115

3 Enter a name for the layer and click on the OK button

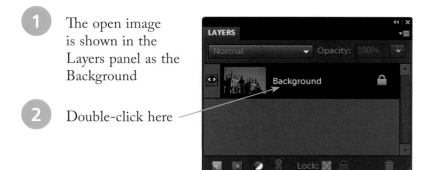

4 The Background layer is converted into a normal layer in the Layers panel

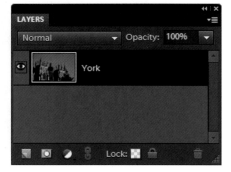

Adding Layers

New blank layers can be added whenever you want to include new content within an image. This could be part of another image that has been copied and pasted, a whole new image, text or an object. To add a new layer:

Don't forget

Text is automatically added on a new layer within an image.

Don't forget

To edit an item on a particular layer, first make sure that the correct layer is selected in the Layers panel. A selected layer is known as the active layer and it is highlighted in the Layers panel with a solid color through it.

1 Click here on the Layers panel

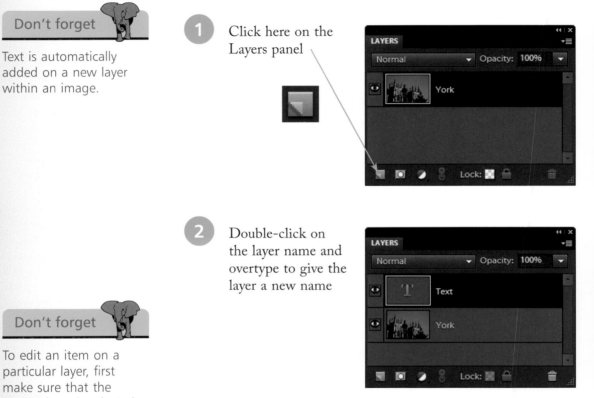

2 Double-click on the layer name and overtype to give the layer a new name

3 With the new layer selected in the Layers panel, add content to the layer. This will be visible over the layer, or layers, below it

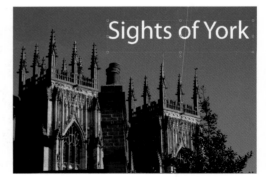

Sights of York

Fill and Adjustment Layers

Fill and adjustment layers can be added to images to give an effect behind or above the main subject. To do this:

1 Open the Layers panel and select a layer. The fill or adjustment layer will be placed directly above the selected layer

Beware

For a Fill layer to be visible behind the main image, the image must have a transparent background. To achieve this, select the main subject. Choose Select>Inverse from the Menu bar and press the Delete key to delete the background. A checkerboard effect should be visible, which denotes that this part of the image is transparent. This only works on layers that have been converted into normal layers, rather than the Background one.

117

2 Click here at the bottom of the Layers panel

3 Select one of the fill or adjustment options. The fill options are Solid Color, Gradient or Pattern Fill

Solid Color...
Gradient...
Pattern...

Levels...
Brightness/Contrast...

Hue/Saturation...
Gradient Map...
Photo Filter...

Invert
Threshold...
Posterize...

Don't forget

The Adjustments panel is used for Levels, Brightness/Contrast, Hue/Saturation, Gradient Map, Photo Filter, Threshold and Posterize.

...cont'd

4 For a Solid
Color, Gradient
or Pattern Fill,
the required fill
is selected from
a dialog box and
this is added to
the selected layer

5 For an adjustment option,
settings can be applied within the
Adjustments panel

6 Once fill and
adjustment settings
have been applied, the
effect can be edited by
changing the opacity.
This is done by dragging this slider

7 The opacity
level
determines
how much of
the image is
visible through
the fill or
adjustment
layer

Working with Layers

Moving layers

The order in which layers are arranged in the Layers panel is known as the stacking order. It is possible to change a layer's position in the stacking order, which affects how it is viewed in the composite image. To do this:

 Click and drag a layer within the Layers panel to change its stacking order

Beware

Layers can be deleted by selecting them and clicking on the Wastebasket icon in the Layers panel. However, this also deletes all of the content on that layer.

Hiding layers

Layers can be hidden while you are working on other parts of an image. However, the layer is still part of the composite image – it has not been removed. To hide a layer:

 Click here so that the eye icon disappears. Click again to reveal it

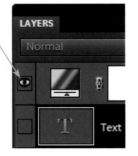

Locking layers

Layers can be locked, so that they cannot accidentally be edited while you are working on other parts of an image. To do this:

 Select a layer and click here so that a padlock appears next to it

Layer Masks

Because layers can be separated within an individual image there is a certain amount of versatility, in terms of how different layers can interact with each other. One of these ways is to create a layer mask. This is a top level layer, through which an area is removed so that the layer below is revealed. To do this:

1 Open an image. It will be displayed as the Background in the Layers panel. Double-click on this to select it

2 Give the layer a new name and click the OK button

3 Access the Content panel (Window> Content from the Menu bar)

4 Select a background and double-click on it to add it to the current image. Initially, this is added below the open image

5 Drag the added layer above the original image (this can also be done by selecting an area in another image, copying it and then pasting it above the existing image)

Beware

Make sure that all layers are converted into normal layers, rather than background ones.

6 The background image now covers the original one

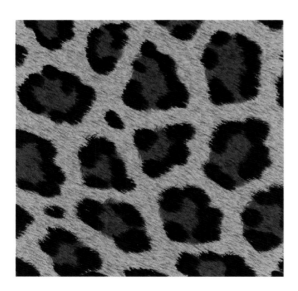

...cont'd

7 Click here to apply a layer mask to the top layer

8 Select the Brush tool from the Toolbox

9 Select a brush size. This can be reasonably large as you will use it to remove part of the top layer

10 Draw on the top layer to remove it and display the image below it

11 In the Layers panel, the area that has been removed is displayed here

Opacity

The opacity of a layer can be set to determine how much of the layer below is visible through the selected layer. To do this:

1 Select a layer either in the Layers panel or by clicking on the relevant item within an image

2 Click here and drag the slider to achieve the required level of opacity. The greater the amount of opacity, the less transparent the selected layer becomes

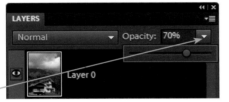

3 The opacity setting determines how much of the background, or the layer below, is visible through the selected one and this can be used to create some interesting artistic effects, including a watermark effect if the opacity is applied to a single layer with nothing behind it

Hot tip

The background behind an image, to which opacity has been applied, can be changed within the Preferences section by selecting Edit>Preferences from the Menu bar and then selecting Transparency and editing the Grid Colors box.

Saving Layers

Once an image has been created using two or more layers, there are two ways in which the composite image can be saved: in a proprietary Photoshop format, in which case individual layers are maintained, or in a general file format, in which case all of the layers will be merged into a single one. The advantage of the former is that individual elements can still be edited within the image, independently of other items. In general, it is good practice to save layered images in both a Photoshop and a non-Photoshop format. To save layered images in a Photoshop format:

Hot tip

Before a layer is saved it is possible to create a composite image consisting of a single layer. To do this, select Layer>Flatten Image from the Menu bar. To merge the existing layer and the one below it, select Layer>Merge Down from the Menu bar, and to merge all visible content (excluding any layers that have been hidden) select Layer> Merge Visible.

1 Select File>Save As from the Menu bar

2 Make sure Photoshop (*.PSD, *.PDD) is selected as the format

3 Make sure the Layers box is checked on

Beware

Layered images that are saved in the Photoshop PSD/PDD format can increase dramatically in file size, compared with the original image or a layered image that has been flattened.

4 Click on the Save button

To save in a non-Photoshop format, select File>Save As from the Menu bar. Select the file format from the Format box and click on the Save button. The Layers box will not be available.

8 Text and Drawing Tools

Elements offers a lot more than just the ability to edit digital images. It also has options for adding and formatting text and creating a variety of graphical objects. This chapter looks at how to add, edit and customize text and also add drawing objects.

Adding and Formatting Text

Text can be added to images in Elements and this can be used to create a wide range of items, such as cards, brochures and posters. To add text to an image:

1 Select the Horizontal or Vertical Type tool from the Toolbox

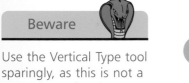

2 Drag on the image with the Type tool to create a text box

3 Make the required formatting selections from the Options bar

Beware

Use the Vertical Type tool sparingly, as this is not a natural way for the eye to read text. Use it with small amounts of text, for effect.

Don't forget

Anti-aliasing is a technique that smooths out the jagged edges that can sometimes appear with text when viewed on a computer monitor. Anti-aliasing is created by adding pixels to the edges of text, so that it blends more smoothly with the background.

Font type   Font style   Font size   Anti-aliased

Formatting (bold, italic, underline and strikethrough)

Alignment   Spacing   Color   Orientation

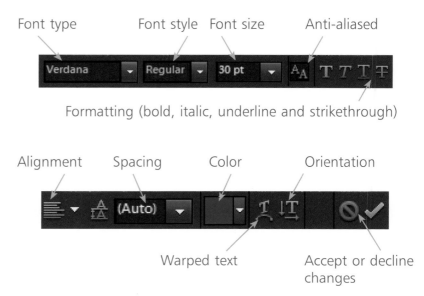

Warped text   Accept or decline changes

4 Type the text onto the image. This is automatically placed on a new layer at the top of the stacking order in the Layers panel

5 To move the text, select it with the Move tool, click and drag it to a new position

To format text that has already been entered:

1 Select a Type tool and drag it over a piece of text to select it

2 Make the changes in the Options bar, as shown in Step 3 on the facing page

Customizing Text

As well as adding standard text, it is also possible to add text to follow a selection, a shape or a custom path. This is done within Full Edit mode.

Adding text to a selection
To add text to a selection within an image:

 Click on the Type tool and select the Text on Selection Tool option

2 Drag over an area of an image to make a selection

3 Click on the green tick to accept the selection

4 Click anywhere on the selection and add text. By default, this will be displayed along the outside of the selection

and we hope you enjoy

5 Format the text in the same way as with standard text

Adding text to a shape

To add text to a shape within an image:

1 Click on the Type tool and select the Text on Shape Tool option

T	Horizontal Type Tool	T
⬆T	Vertical Type Tool	T
T	Horizontal Type Mask Tool	T
T	Vertical Type Mask Tool	T
T	Text on Selection Tool	T
T	Text on Shape Tool	T

2 Click here in the Options bar to select a shape

Ellipse ▼

Rectangle
Rounded Rectangle
Ellipse
Polygon
Heart
Speech Bubble
Butterfly

3 Drag over an area of an image to create a shape

4 Click anywhere on the shape and add text. Click on the green tick as in Step 3 on the previous page

5 Format the text in the same way as with standard text

...cont'd

Adding text to a custom path

Text can also be added to a custom path that you draw on an image. To do this:

 Open the image onto which you want to create text on a custom path

 Click on the Type tool and select the Text on Custom Path Tool option

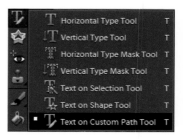

 Draw a custom path on the image

4 Click on the green tick to accept the text path

5 Click anywhere on the custom path and add text

6 Format the text in the  same way as with standard text

7 Click on the Refine Path tool in the Options bar. This activates the markers along the custom path

8 Drag the markers to move the position of the custom path

Beware

If there is too much text on a custom path it can become jumbled, particularly if you adjust the markers on the path.

9 The custom path can be used to position text in a variety of ways around objects or people

Distorting Text

In addition to producing standard text, it is also possible to create some dramatic effects by distorting text. To do this:

Hot tip

It is possible to select the distort options before text is added.

1 Enter plain text and select it by dragging a Type tool over it

Vegas at night

2 Click the Create Warped Text button on the Options bar

3 Click here and select one of the options in the Warp Text dialog box. Click OK

Warp Text

Style: None

None
Arc
Arc Lower
Arc Upper
Arch
Bulge
Shell Lower
Shell Upper
Flag

OK
Cancel

Beware

Use text distortion sparingly, as it can become annoying if it is overdone.

4 The selected effect is applied to the text

Text and Shape Masks

Text Masks can be used to reveal an area of an image showing through the text. This can be used to produce eye-catching headings and slogans. To do this:

 Select the Horizontal or Vertical Type Mask tool from the Toolbox

 Click on an image, enter and format text as you would for normal text. A red mask is applied to the image when the mask text is entered

Hot tip

Text Mask effects work best if the text used is fairly large in size. In some cases it is a good idea to use bold text, as this is wider than standard text.

133

 Press Enter or click the Move tool to border the mask text with dots

...cont'd

 4 Select Edit>Copy from the Menu bar

5 Select File>New from the Menu bar and create a new file

6 Select Edit>Paste from the Menu bar to paste the text mask into the new file

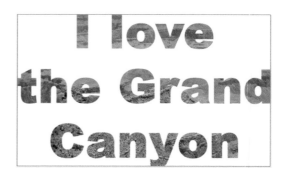

134

Cookie Cutter masks

A similar effect can be created with shape masks by using the Cookie Cutter tool:

1 Select the Cookie Cutter tool in the Toolbox and click here to select a particular style in the Options bar

2 Drag on an image to create a cut-out effect

Adding Shapes

Another way to add extra style to your images is through the use of shapes. There are several types of symmetrical shapes that can be added to images, and also a range of custom ones. To add shapes to an image:

1 Click and hold the Rectangle tool in the Toolbox

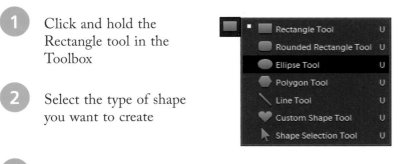

2 Select the type of shape you want to create

3 Click and drag on the image to create the selected shape

Don't forget

The tools for creating shapes are also available from the Options bar, when the Rectangle tool (or any related tool from this toolset) is selected.

135

4 If you want to change the color of a shape, click here in the Options bar and select a new color. This can either be done before the shape is created or it can be used to edit the color of an existing shape, when selected with the Move tool

...cont'd

Custom shapes

Custom shapes can be used to add pre-designed graphical objects, rather than just symmetrical shapes. To do this:

 Select the Custom Shape tool from the Toolbox

 Click here in the Options bar to view the different custom shapes

Click once on a shape to select it

Click here to view other categories of shapes

Click and drag on an image to add a custom shape

Layer Styles

When plain text and objects are added to images, they appear as two-dimensional items. If you want to give them a 3-D effect, this can be achieved through the use of the Styles and Effects panel.

To do this:

1 Select Window>Effects from the Menu bar

2 Click here to access the Layer Styles

3 Click here to access different styles

4 Select an object, or a piece of text, with the Move tool and click once on a layer style to apply that style to the selected item in the image

Don't forget

Layer Styles can be applied to symmetrical objects and custom ones.

Hot tip

The Drop Shadow styles are a good option for adding emphasis to textual items, such as headings. However, don't over-use them.

Paint Bucket Tool

The Paint Bucket tool can be used to add a solid color to a selection or an object. To do this:

 Select an area within an image or select an object

 Select the Paint Bucket tool from the Toolbox

Don't forget

For more information on working with color, see pages 143–144.

138

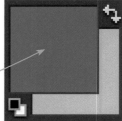

Click here in the Toolbox to access the Color Picker for changing the currently selected color

Click once on the selected area or object to change its color to the one loaded in the Paint Bucket tool

Gradient Tool

The Gradient tool can be used to add a gradient fill to a selection or an object. To do this:

1 Select an area in an image or select an object

Beware

If no selection is made for a gradient fill, the effect will be applied to the entire selected layer.

2 Select the Gradient tool from the Toolbox

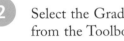

3 Click here in the Options bar to select preset gradient fills

4 Click on a gradient style to apply it as the default

Hot tip

The default gradient effect in the Options bar is created with the currently selected foreground and background colors within the Toolbox.

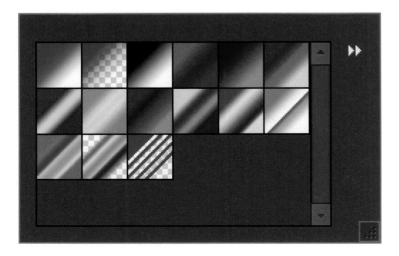

...cont'd

5 Click here in the Options bar to access the Gradient Editor dialog box

6 Click and drag the sliders to change the amount of a particular color in the gradient

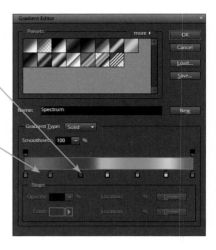

7 Click along here to add a new color marker. Click on the OK button

140

8 Click an icon in the Options bar to select a gradient style

9 Click and drag within the original selection to specify the start and end points of the gradient effect

Brush and Pencil Tools

The Brush and Pencil tools work in a similar way and can be used to create lines of varying thickness and style. To do this:

 Select the Brush tool or the Pencil tool from the Toolbox

2 Select the required options from the Options bar

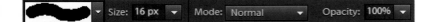

3 Click and drag to create lines on an image. (The lines are placed directly on the image. To add lines without altering the background image, add a new layer above the background and add the lines on this layer. They will then be visible over the background.)

141

Don't forget

The Mode options for the Brush and Pencil tools are similar to those for blending layers together. They include options such as Darken, Lighten, Soft Light and Difference. Each of these enables the line to blend with the image below it.

Don't forget

The Brush and Pencil tools are very similar in the way they function, except that the Brush tool has more options and can create more subtle effects.

Impressionist Brush Tool

The Impressionist Brush tool can be used to create a dappled effect over an image, similar to that of an impressionist painting. To do this:

1 Select the Impressionist Brush tool from the Toolbox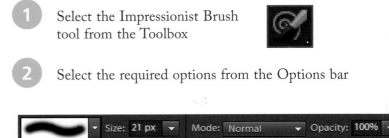

2 Select the required options from the Options bar

Size: **21 px** ▼ Mode: Normal ▼ Opacity: **100%** ▼

3 Click and drag over an image to create an impressionist effect

Working with Color

All of the text and drawing tools make extensive use of color. Elements provides a number of methods for selecting colors, and also for working with them.

Foreground and background colors

At the bottom of the Toolbox there are two colored squares. These represent the currently selected foreground and background colors. The foreground color, which is the most frequently used, is the one that is applied to drawing objects, such as fills and lines, and also text. The background color is used for items, such as gradient fills, and for areas that have been removed with the Eraser tool.

Foreground color   Swap foreground and background colors

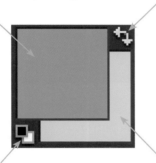

Set foreground to black and background to white   Background color

Hot tip

Whenever the foreground or background color squares are clicked on, the Eyedropper tool is automatically activated. This can be used to select a color from anywhere on your screen, instead of using the Color Picker.

143

Color Picker

The Color Picker can be used to select a new color for the foreground or background color. To do this:

1 Click once on the foreground or the background color square, as required

Hot tip

If you are going to be using images on the Web, check on the Only Web Colors box. This will display a different range of colors, which are known as Web-safe colors. This means that they will appear the same on any type of web browser.

Don't forget

When the cursor is moved over a color in the Color Swatches panel, the tooltip displays the color's hexadecimal value. This is a six character sequence which displays the color in terms of the amount of red, green and blue it contains. Hexadecimal color values are made up of three groups of two characters and they consist of numbers 0–9 and letters A–F.

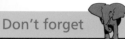

2 In the Color Picker, click to select a color

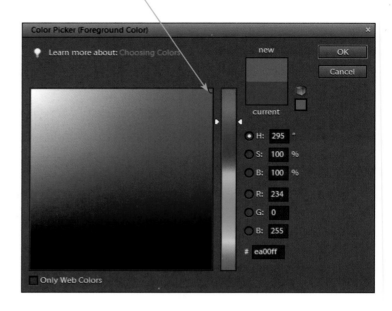

3 Click on the OK button

Color Swatches panel

The Color Swatches panel can be used to access different color panels that can then be used to select the foreground and background colors. To do this:

1 Select Window>Color Swatches from the Menu bar

2 Click here to access the available panels

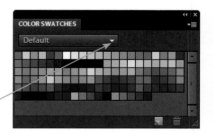

9 Artistic Effects

Adding special effects is one of the fun things about digital images. This chapter shows how to add artwork and create stunning effects for your photos to give them the "wow" factor to stun family and friends.

About Content and Effects

Applying special effects can be one of the most satisfying parts of digital image editing: it is quick and the results can be dramatic. Elements has a range of Content and Effects that can be applied to images. To use these:

Don't forget

The Content and Effects panels can only be accessed from the Editor, not the Organizer.

1 In the Editor, select Window>Content or Effects from the Menu bar to access the Content and Effects panels

2 Within the Content panel click here to select a category for a particular topic

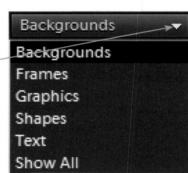

3 Click here to see all of the options for a particular category

Applying Effects

To apply special effects to an open image in the Editor:

1 Select the required item in the Effects panel

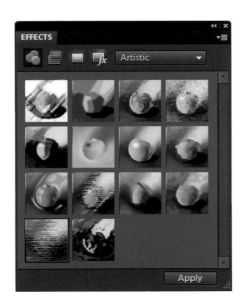

2 Click on the Apply button

3 Some effects, such as Filters, have additional dialog boxes in which a variety of settings can be specified in relation to how the effect operates and appears

Artwork

The Content panel can be used to add graphical elements to images. This can be done either to existing images or to a blank file, onto which other content can be added. To do this:

Hot tip

The Blank File command can be used to add content to an empty file, such as here, or if you want to paste an item that has been copied from another image.

1 In the Editor, select File>New>Blank File from the Menu bar

2 Click here in the Content panel and click on Backgrounds

3 Select a background from the Content panel

Beware

If a background is added to an existing image, the image will be obscured by the background.

4 Click on the Apply button or double-click on the background

5 The background is added to the blank file

6 Repeat step 3, but select a Frame option. This will then enable you to add an image, by clicking here or dragging an open image from the Project Bin

Hot tip

The order in which items appear in the image can be altered by changing the order of the layers in the Layers panel.

7 Repeat Step 3, but select the Graphics option to add a graphical element

8 Repeat Step 3, but select the Shapes option to add a 2D shape

Hot tip

If you save the final image as a Photoshop file (.PSD; .PDD) you will still be able to open the image and edit each of the individual elements. However, if you save it as a JPEG, you will not be able to edit any of the artwork elements.

9 Save the final image in the same way as any other file

Smart Brush Tool Effects

The Smart Brush tool can be used to create a variety of effects for either the foreground or the background of an image. To do this:

 Open an image to which you would like to apply the Smart Brush tool effects

 Select the Smart Brush tool

Select an area of the image with the Smart Brush tool by dragging over the required area

Click here on the Options bar to access the options for the Smart Brush picker

Click here to view the available categories

The selection is applied to the area selected in Step 3

Background Effects

Select the background and apply a Smart Brush effect (in this example it is Black Checks from the Textures category):

Foreground Effects

Select the foreground and apply a Smart Brush effect (in this example it is Spooky from the Special Effects category):

Once a selection has been made, icons appear to add or delete from the selection. To do this, click on one of the icons and then drag over the area that you want to add or delete.

Depth of Field

Depth of field is a photographic technique where part of a photo is deliberately blurred, for artistic effect. Traditionally, this has been done through camera settings, but in Elements the same effect can be created within the Guided Edit section. To do this:

1 Open the image to which you want to add the depth of field effect

2 Access the Guided Edit section. In the Lens Effects section, click on the Depth of Field link

3 Click on the Simple button

4 Click on the Add Blur button to add a blurred effect to the whole image

5 Click on the Gradient Tool button

6 Drag on the image, covering the area that you want to appear in focus

153

7 Drag this slider to increase the amount of blur of the area that is not in focus

8 Click on the Done button

Line Drawings

By using the Guided Edit function there are a number of artistic special effects that can be applied to images in a straightforward, step-by-step process. One of these is converting images into line drawings. To do this:

 Open the image you want to convert into a line drawing

 Access the Guided Edit section. In the Photography Effects section, click on the Line Drawing link

▼ Photography Effects

Line Drawing   >

3 The process is detailed with each step and a description of what it does. Click on the Pencil Sketch button

1. Click Pencil Sketch.

Pencil Sketch

(Optional) A nice effect can be achieved by bringing back a bit of the original photo's color. This is accomplished by reducing the opacity of the duplicate layer with the Pencil Sketch effect. In this guided edit, we're going to reduce the opacity between 75 and 80%.

4 Click on the Adjust Layer Opacity button to make the lines in the drawing darker

> 2. Click Adjust Layer Opacity.
>
> Adjust Layer Opacity

5 Click on the Levels button to increase the overall contrast in the image. This can improve the detail in the image

> 3. Click Levels.
>
> Levels

6 Click on the Done button to complete the process

> Done

7 The line drawing effect is applied to the image. This can then be saved as a new image

Hot tip

Once a line drawing has been created, and saved, it can then be edited further in Full Edit mode. This can be used to fine-tune the levels, or increase the brightness and contrast.

Photographic Effects

Within the Guided Edit function there are a number of photographic effects that can be added to images. These have been developed by photographers over the years and they are now available within Elements.

Lomo Camera Effect

This is an effect that puts a vignette around an image and creates a more vibrantly colored image. To do this:

Don't forget

The Lomo camera effect comes from a Russian company, of the same name, founded in 1914. They made optical equipment, including cameras. Unfortunately the standard of these was poor, resulting in overly-saturated colors, questionable exposures and darkening around the edges of images (vignetting). However, this style has become popular with photographers and it can now be reproduced in Elements.

1 Open the image you want to convert into a Lomo Effect

2 Access the Guided Edit section. In the Photography Effects section, click on the Lomo Camera Effect link

▼ Photography Effects
Line Drawing
Lomo Camera Effect

3 Click on the Cross Process Image link. This applies the color effect to the image

1. Click the Cross Process button to give your image that Lomo camera look.

Cross Process Image

4 Click on the Apply Vignette button. This applies the vignette effect to the whole image. Click on the button again to make the effect more defined

> 2. Add a Vignette to your image to finalize the Lomo camera effect.
>
> **Apply Vignette**
>
> *Tip: Click again to intensify effect*

5 Click on the Done button

Done

Orton Effect

This is another photographic effect that can give a soft-focus appearance to an image. This is also done within the Photography Effects section. To do this, access the Orton Effect link in the same way as for the Lomo Camera Effect:

1 Click on the Add Orton Effect button to add the main effect

2 Drag the sliders to edit the effect on the image

3 Click on the Done button

Add Orton Effect

Increase Blur

Increase Noise

Apply Brightness

Don't forget

The Orton Effect was invented by the photographer Michael Orton. It involves overlaying two images of the same subject, with different exposures and one in focus and one out of focus. This results in a soft-focus final image.

Out of Bounds

A new special effect that has been added to Elements 10 is called Out of Bounds. This can be used to display a section of an image without the rest of the original photo. This works best when there is one part of the image that obviously sticks out from the rest, such as part of a building, or someone's arm or leg. To create the Out of Bounds effect:

 Open an image that has an element that will naturally stick out from the rest

Don't forget

As long as it is a defined area, anything can be used to appear without the rest of the image.

2 Access the Guided Edit section. In the Photo Play section, click on the Out of Bounds link

▼ Photo Play

Out Of Bounds   >
Picture Stack   >
Pop Art   >
Reflection   >

3 Click on the Add a Frame button

> **Frame:**
>
> 1a. Click the Add Frame button to get started.
>
> **Add a Frame**

4 A default frame is added to the image. This can be sized by dragging the buttons situated around the border. It can be moved by clicking on the border and then dragging it into the required position. The area of the frame is the one that will form the main part of the final image

Don't forget

The frame contains the area that will be the main part of the image, not the Out of Bounds selection.

159

5 Hold down Shift+Ctrl+Alt to add perspective to the frame. This can be done by dragging the corner position buttons and also those in the middle of each side

6 Click on the green arrow to apply the changes to the frame

...cont'd

 7 The frame is displayed, with the rest of the image grayed-out

8 Click on the Quick Selection Tool button

Quick Selection Tool

9 Drag over the area that will appear outside the main image

Hot tip

Zoom in on the area to be selected so that you can do this with greater precision and accuracy.

Click on the Create Out of Bounds button

Create Out of Bounds

 The area selected in Step 9 now appears on its own, outwith the area created by the frame

Use the Stylize buttons to add a drop shadow around the final image

Stylize:
5. Add a Shadow to your image to add some depth

Small   Medium   Large

6. Add a Gradient Background to finalize your image.

Add a Gradient

Click on the Add a Gradient button to add a background gradient to the final image

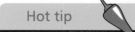

Hot tip

A gradient can be added by clicking on the Add a Gradient button and selecting a gradient style in the dialog box.

Click on the Done button to complete the process

Done

Pop Art

One of the best known artistic techniques is pop art, made famous by Andy Warhol in the 1960s. Now, it is possible to create your own pop art images with Elements. To do this:

 Open the image you want to convert to pop art

 Access the Guided Edit section. In the Photo Play section, click on the Pop Art link

 Select a style for your pop art creation

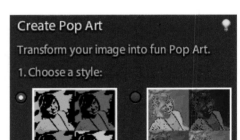

 Click on the Convert Image Mode button

5   Click on the Add Color button

> **3. Add a Color fill adjustment layer**
>
> Add Color

6   The image is converted into a single pop art image

Don't forget

The colors for the Pop Art effect are created automatically when the effect is applied.

7   Click on the Duplicate Image button

> **4. Duplicate image with different pop colors**
>
> Duplicate Image

8   The image is converted into the iconic pop art style, with four differently colored versions of the same image

9   Click on the Done button to complete the process

> Done

Reflections

Reflections of an image can be one of the most satisfying photographic effects. Images reflected in water, or on a clear surface, can create a very artistic and calming effect. However, it can be difficult to get the perfect reflection when taking an original photo. To help overcome this Elements has a Guided Edit that can create the effect for you. To do this:

 Open the image you want to use for the reflection. If possible, use one with some objects in the foreground

Beware

If you select an image that does not have enough detail in the foreground, the join with the reflected image may appear too severe and slightly unnatural.

 Access the Guided Edit section. In the Photo Play section, click on the Reflection link

▼ Photo Play

Out Of Bounds   >
Picture Stack   >
Pop Art   >
Reflection   >

Click on the Add Reflection button

1. Click the Add Reflection button to get started.

Add Reflection

4 The reflection effect is applied to the image

5 Depending on the type of reflection you are creating you can add a background color by selecting the Eyedropper tool and clicking on the Fill Background button

2. Use the Eyedropper tool to choose a background color for your reflection.

 Eyedropper tool

3. Fill the background with your selected color.

Fill Background

Beware

If a background color is used, this will be applied to the reflected image. However, this step does not have to be used.

6 Select the type of reflection effect you want to create

4. Apply an effect to make your reflection more realistic.

Floor Reflection

Glass Reflection

Water Reflection

...cont'd

 7 Each option has different dialog boxes which can be used to set the amount. Click on the OK button to apply the selected effect

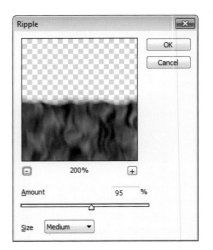

 8 The effect is applied to the reflected half of the image

 9 Additional options can be applied to fine-tune the selected effect further

 10 Click on the Done button to complete the process

Done

10 Sharing and Creating

This chapter shows how you can share images creatively and also use and edit them in artistic projects.

Saving Images for the Web

One of the issues for images that are going to be shared online is file size. This must be small enough so that the images can be downloaded quickly on a web page, or as an attachment in an email. To assist in this, Elements has a function for saving images in different formats and also altering the quality settings for each format. This enables you to balance the quality and file size, so that you have the optimum image for use online. To do this:

 Open an image in the Editor and select File>Save for Web from the Menu bar

 The original image is shown on the left of the Save for Web window

Select options for optimizing the image here

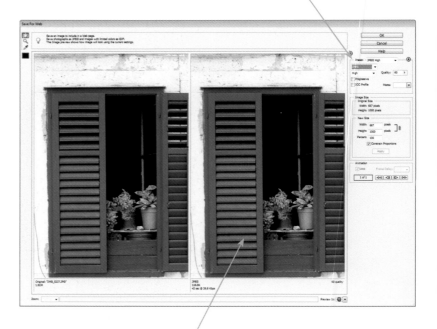

 The preview of the optimized image is shown here, once the settings have been applied

5 The new file size and download time at a specified speed are shown below the image in the right hand panel

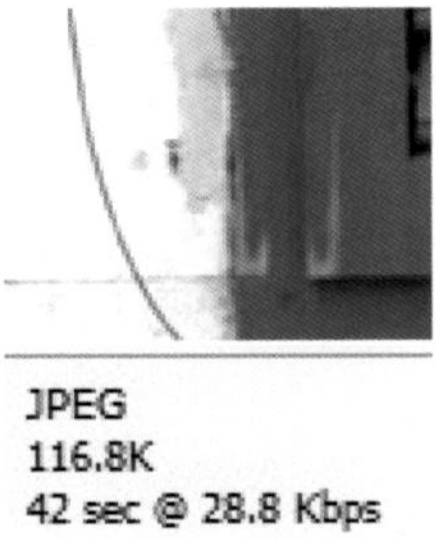

JPEG
116.8K
42 sec @ 28.8 Kbps

Beware

In Elements, the compression setting and the quality setting are linked, so that when one is altered the other is changed automatically.

6 Click here to select a file type and level of compression

OK

Cancel

Help

Preset: Custom

JPEG

Medium   Quality: 40

Progressive

ICC Profile   Matte:

7 Click here to select a quality setting

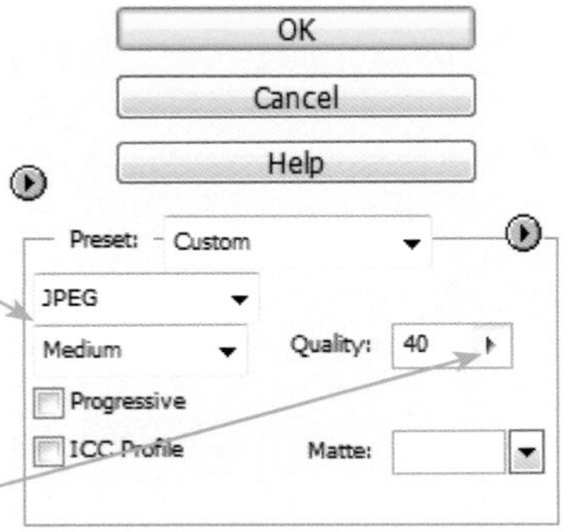

8 Enter new dimensions here to change the physical size of the image

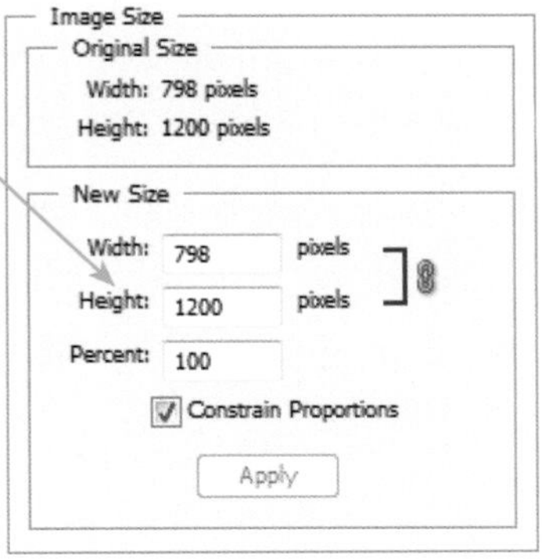

Image Size
Original Size
Width: 798 pixels
Height: 1200 pixels

New Size
Width: 798 pixels
Height: 1200 pixels
Percent: 100

Constrain Proportions

Apply

Don't forget

Even low-quality images can look good on web pages, as computer monitors are more forgiving in their image output than hard copy printing is.

9 Click on the OK button

OK

10 In the Save Optimized As window, save the image with a new name so that the original remains intact

Save Optimized As

File name: DSC_0007-1_copy

169

About Share Mode

Share mode enables you to output your images in a variety of ways, and also send them to friends and family in different formats. Some of these involve third party services and these will vary depending on your own location. Also, some of the options offered through the Share mode require the video editing program, Elements Premiere. The standard options within Share mode are:

- Online Album. This can be used to display your photos online, using the available third party suppliers

- E-mail Attachments. This can be used to attach photos to emails via your email program

- Photo Mail. This can be used to produce creative email messages with your photos

- Burn Video DVD/BluRay. This requires Elements Premiere

- Online Video Sharing. This requires Elements Premiere

- Mobile Phones and Players. This requires Elements Premiere

- Share to Flickr and Facebook. This can be used to share images to social media sites

- Share with Kodak Easyshare Gallery. This can be used to share images on online photo site

- Share video to YouTube. This can be used to upload videos to YouTube

To use Share mode

Don't forget

Share Mode has additional options to create a PDF Slide Show and share with Adobe Photoshop Showcase, which is an online Adobe service for image sharing.

170

1 In either the Editor or the Organizer, click on the Share tab and select an option

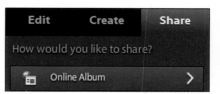

2 Select the options for how you want to share the selected item

3 Add content to be shared (either by selecting it initially or by dragging it into the Content panel)

Don't forget

Each Share option has a slightly different wizard, but the basic process is the same for each one.

4 Format the content using the wizards and templates within the Share section

5 Click on the Done button to share your photos with the selected format

Sharing on Facebook

With the explosion in popularity of social networking sites such as Facebook, it is not a surprise that there are now a number of applications available for people to upload photos to their own pages on these sites. Within Elements it is now possible to upload photos directly to Facebook. To do this:

1 Open a photo in the Editor, or select it in the Organizer. Select the Share tab and click on the Share to Facebook option

2 You will be asked to authorize your account so that Elements can become an approved method for uploading your Facebook photos. Check on the Download Facebook Friend List to allow Elements to use your Facebook friends for face recognition when searching for images

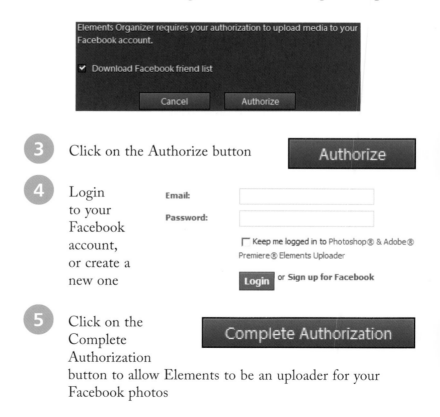

Elements Organizer requires your authorization to upload media to your Facebook account.

✔ Download Facebook friend list

Cancel   Authorize

3 Click on the Authorize button

4 Login to your Facebook account, or create a new one

Email:
Password:
☐ Keep me logged in to Photoshop® & Adobe® Premiere® Elements Uploader
Login or Sign up for Facebook

5 Click on the Complete Authorization button to allow Elements to be an uploader for your Facebook photos

About Create Mode

Image editing programs have now evolved to a point where there is almost as much emphasis on using images creatively as there is on editing them. Elements has an excellent range of options for displaying your images in some stunningly creative ways, called, appropriately enough, Create mode. These can be saved in the Organizer for viewing or sharing. The standard options within Create mode are:

- Photo Prints. This can be used to print photos locally on your own printer, or using an online service

- Photo Book. This creates a selection of formatted images that can be printed in a presentational book

- Greeting Cards. This creates your own personalized cards

- Photo Calendar. This creates your own personalized calendars

- Photo Collage. This can be used to assemble several images

- Slide Show. This creates a slide show of selected images

- Instant Movie. This requires Elements Premiere

- DVD with Menu. This can be used to create a DVD of your photos and video, with an interactive menu at the front

- CD Jacket. This can be used to create customized CD covers

To use Create mode:

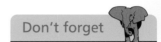

 In either the Editor or the Organizer, click on the Create button

Select one of the Create options

...cont'd

3 In the dialog window for the Create option select a size at which the creation will be printed

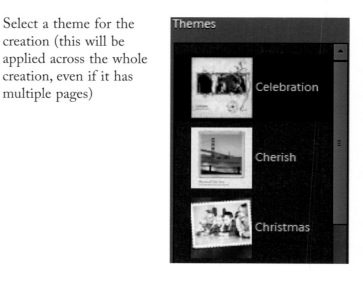

4 Select a theme for the creation (this will be applied across the whole creation, even if it has multiple pages)

5 A preview of the layout for the creation is shown in the right-hand panel

6 Click on the OK button

OK

7 Click on the Pages tab to add more pages to a creation. This is done with the green plus sign

8 Click on the Layout tab to select one of the predesigned layouts

9 Click on the Artwork tab to add backgrounds, frames and graphics to the pages within the creation

10 Click on the Text tab to select options for formatting text within the creation

Don't forget

Text blocks can be used to add your own messages to your photos within creations.

175

...cont'd

Hot tip

Some Creations can be printed via online services by opening them and selecting the Create> Photo Prints option and then choosing an available online service.

Beware

Because of the amount of content in them, and the format in which they are saved, Creations can have very large file sizes.

11 Once a creation is completed, click on the Print button to print it on your own printer

Print

12 Click on the Done button to complete the creation. It will then still need to be saved within Elements

Done

13 Once a project has been saved it is displayed in the Organizer. This means that it can then be opened again and edited if required

14 A project file is denoted by this icon in the top right corner

Editing Creations

By default, Creations are produced using wizards and templates within the Create area. This makes it straightforward in terms of producing Creations, but without the power of Full Edit mode. However, in Elements 10 you can now select an Advanced mode so that you can use all of the standard editing tools on the parts of your creation. To do this:

1 In Create mode, there are limited independent editing options. The editing is done within the Create section

177

Don't forget

When an item is edited within Advanced Mode, this is done independently of the other elements of the creation, which remain untouched.

2 Click on the Switch to Advanced Mode button

Switch to Advanced Mode

3 The full Tools toolbox becomes available

...cont'd

Don't forget

When in Advanced Mode, the normal Create options are still available.

Hot tip

Viewing the elements of a creation in the Layers panel is a great way to understand the structure of the creation and also to see how layers interact with each other.

4 Select an image within the creation so that it can be edited

5 Any editing effects can be applied, such as adjusting the hue and saturation

6 The Layers panel allows you to examine the structure of the creation. Check off these boxes to hide elements of the creation

7 Click on the Switch to Basic Mode button to return to the regular Create mode

Switch to Basic Mode

11 Printing Images

This chapter shows how to size images for printing, and how to print them in a variety of formats.

Print Size

Before you start printing images in Elements, it is important to ensure that they are going to be produced at the required size. Since the pixels within an image are not a set size, the printed dimensions of an image can be altered according to your needs. This is done by specifying how many pixels are used within each inch of the image. The more pixels per inch (ppi) then the higher the quality of the printed image, but the smaller in size it will be.

To set the print size of an image:

Don't forget

The higher the resolution in the Document Size section of the dialog, the greater the quality, but the smaller the size of the printed image.

Hot tip

The output size for a printed image can be worked out by dividing the pixel dimensions (the width and height) by the resolution. So if the width is 2560, the height 1920 and the resolution 300, the printed image will be roughly 8 inches by 6 inches.

1 Open an image and select Image>Resize>Image Size from the Menu bar

2 Uncheck the Resample Image box. This will ensure that the physical image size, i.e. the number of pixels in the image, remains unchanged when the resolution is changed

3 The current resolution and document size (print size) are displayed here

4 Enter a new figure in the Resolution box (here the resolution has been increased from 72 to 300). This affects the Document size, i.e. the size at which the image prints

Don't forget

As long as the Resample box is unchecked, changing the output resolution has no effect on the actual number of pixels in an image.

Print Functions

The Print functions in Elements can be accessed from the Menu bar in either the Editor or the Organizer, by selecting File>Print. Also, all of the print functions can be selected directly from the Create section. To print to your local printer using this method:

1 Select and image in either the Editor or the Organizer, click on the Create button and click on the Photo Prints button

2 Click on the Print with Local Printer button

3 The main print window displays the default option for how the printed image will appear and also options for changing the properties of the print

4 Click the Add button to include more images in the current print job, or select an image and click on the Remove button to exclude it

...cont'd

5 Use these options to rotate an image for printing, change its size, or position

6 Click here to select a destination printer to which you want to send your print

1 Select Printer:

Dell Laser Printer 1720dn ▼

7 Click on the Change Settings button to change the properties for your own local printer

2 Printer Settings:

Paper Type: Printer Setting

Print Quality: 600 DPI

Tray: Automatically Select

Change Settings....

8 Click here to select the paper size for printing

3 Select Paper Size:

A4 ▼

9 Click here to select the print type i.e. the layout of the image you are printing

4 Select Type of Print:

Individual Prints ▼

10 Click here to select the size at which you want your image to be printed

5 Select Print Size:

10.2cm x 15.2cm ▼

☐ Crop to Fit

11 Click on the Print button to print your image with the settings selected above

Print...

Print Layouts

Rather than just offering the sole function of printing a single image on a sheet of paper, Elements has two options that can be used when printing images, which can help reduce the number of sheets of paper used.

Picture Package

This can be used to print out copies of different images on a single piece of paper. To do this:

1 Select an image in either the Editor or the Organizer, click on the Create button and click on the Print Picture Package button

2 The layout for the Picture Package is displayed in the main print window

3 Under Select a Layout, select how many images you want on a page and, if required, select a type of frame for the printed images.

Hot tip

When buying a printer, choose one that has borderless printing. This means that it can print to the very edge of the page. This is particularly useful for items, such as files, produced as a Picture Package.

183

Don't forget

The Picture Package function is a useful one for printing images in a combination of sizes, such as for family portraits.

...cont'd

Contact Sheets

This can be used to create and print thumbnail versions of a large number of images. To do this:

1 Select an image in either the Editor or the Organizer, click on the Create button and click on the Print Contact Sheet button

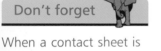

Don't forget

When a contact sheet is created, new thumbnail images are generated. The original images are unaffected.

2 The layout for the Contact Sheet is displayed in the main Print window

3 Click under Select Type of Print and select the number of columns to be displayed on the contact sheet

Online Prints

Online printing of digital images is now firmly established and it is an excellent way of getting high quality, economical, prints without leaving the comfort of your own home.

 Open an image, or images, in either the Editor, or select them in the Organizer. Click on the Create button

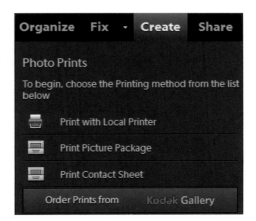

Hot tip

When printing images, either online or on your own printer, make sure that they have been captured at the highest resolution setting on your camera, to ensure the best printed quality.

2 There are options for printing images on your own printer, and also services for online prints. These will be specific to your own location. When you click on one of the services you will be taken to their website, from where you will be able to order your online prints. You will have to register for the site initially, which will be free. Most services will also have an option for uploading your photos, so that they can be viewed online

185

Creating PDF Files

PDF (Portable Document Format) is a file format that is used to maintain the original formatting and style of a document, so that it can be viewed on a variety of different devices and types of computers. In general, it is usually used for documents that contain text and images, such as information pamphlets, magazine features and chapters from books. However, image files, such as JPEGs, can also be converted into PDF and this can be done within Elements without the need for any other special software. To do this:

Don't forget

PDF files are an excellent way to share files so that other people can print them. All that is required is a copy of Adobe Acrobat Reader, which is bundled with most software packages on computers, or can be downloaded from the Adobe website at: **www.adobe.com**

1 Open a file and select File>Save As from the Menu bar

2 Select a destination folder and make sure the format is set to Photoshop PDF. Then click Save

| File name: | kosovo10.pdf | ▼ | Save |
| Format: | Photoshop PDF (*.PDF;*.PDP) | ▼ | Cancel |

3 The PDF file is created and can be opened in Adobe Acrobat or Elements

Index